Western Witness
Presbyterians in the Area of the Synod of Manitoba
1700-1885

WESTERN

WITNESS

THE PRESBYTERIANS IN
THE AREA OF THE
SYNOD OF MANITOBA

1700-1885

DR. JAMES MARNOCH

Cover design by Terry Gallagher/Doowah Design Inc.
Author photo by McMaster Studios

All illustrations and photos (except Kildonan Cemetery and Old Kildonan Presbyterian Church, J. Marnoch) courtesy of Provincial Archives of Manitoba.

Published with the assistance of the Manitoba Arts Council and The Canada Council.

Printed and bound in Canada by Hignell Printing Ltd.

Canadian Cataloguing in Publication Data

Marnoch, James, 1913–

    Western witness

    Includes bibliographical references and index.
    ISBN 0-920486-03-7

1. Presbyterians – Northwest, Canadian – History.
2. Presbyterians – Manitoba – History. 3. Presbyterian Church in Canada. Synod of Manitoba and the North-West Territories – History. I. Title

BX9002.M3M37 1994   285'.2712'09   C94-920252-5

Watson & Dwyer Publishing
P.O. Box 86, 905 Corydon Avenue, Winnipeg, MB R3M 3S3

"You will be witnesses for me in Jerusalem, in all of Judea and Samaria, and to the end of the earth."
Acts 1:8

TABLE OF CONTENTS

INTRODUCTION

In the subtitle, the "Area" referred to is Western Canada from Lake Superior to the Pacific Ocean. The Synod of Manitoba does not exist until the end of this story.

In the Presbyterian Church, a Synod is the Court which groups several Presbyteries. A Presbytery is the more local Court which groups congregations. Congregations are the voluntary groups of individuals.

This story tells of individuals; of the first congregation in the area; of the first Presbytery; and finally, of the first Synod.

That is the shape of the Church for Presbyterians; but they are to be found in all walks of life. Whatever their lot, they have this in common, that for many generations they have learned the Shorter Catechism, and have been influenced by it. Its Bible teaching begins with the question "What is the chief end of Man?" The answer becomes, whether consciously or unconsciously, the priority of their lives: "Man's chief end is to glorify God, and to enjoy Him forever."

Other Christians express the same great truth in different ways. Presbyterians, too, are tending to find different expressions for this, but the priority remains the same.

CHAPTER ONE

THE FIRST PRESBYTERIANS, 1700-1810

THE ORCADIANS

They referred to themselves as Orcadians. The Hudson's Bay Company called them Orkneymen. They were the young men of the Orkney Islands off the north shore of Scotland. In the earliest years of the eighteenth century the Hudson's Bay Company employed them as staff for the fur trading posts around the shores of Hudson Bay. The northern climate from which they came made them suitable. The poverty of their homeland made them willing. They sailed in Company ships from their port of Stromness across the Atlantic and through the Hudson Straight to their posts at the mouths of the great rivers flowing into Hudson Bay. Those who went to the Churchill, the Nelson and the Severn Rivers were the first Presbyterians to live and work in the vast area which later became known, in Presbyterian terms, as the Synod of Manitoba.

For fifty years young Orcadians served their terms at these posts, then returned home with their savings, to be replaced by others from their Islands. During the eighteenth century about seventy men came each year. By the end of the century "of the Company's five hundred and thirty men in North America almost four out of five were Orkneymen."[1]

During the first half of the eighteenth century the Hudson's Bay men stayed at their posts, while the "Indians" travelled long distances to trade their furs. The departing Orcadians sometimes left behind, as a living legacy, their children by "Indian" women.

THE NOR'WESTERS

During the latter half of the eighteenth century the fur trading pattern was drastically altered. The Hudson's Bay men were forced to leave their Bay-shore posts and travel up the rivers in order to meet strong new competition.

For many years French explorers and fur traders from New France (Quebec) had been intercepting Indians on their way to Hudson Bay without causing the Company too much concern. However after the British conquest and the Treaty of 1763 the French withdrew from the West. Like the Orcadians, the French had also left a legacy—the Métis, the roving, volatile buffalo hunters.

The places of the French were soon taken by adventurous and aggressive men of many ethnic origins. Some were disbanded British soldiers. Others were experienced British traders who left the United States after Independence. Many of them were young men of the Scottish Highlands and Islands who came to Canada to make their fortune. To these last, driven by poverty, desperation, and the breakdown of their society after the defeat of Bonnie Prince Charlie at Culloden in 1746, the fur trade with its potential rewards was a magnet.

Aided by the indispensable skill and knowledge of French voyageurs, the new traders invaded the West from Montreal. They traced the great rivers and explored westward and northward until even the Athabasca River area served their fur trade. They thought of themselves as being inheritors of the old French trading empire, and dared to challenge the validity of the Hudson's Bay Company Charter of 1670. They reached the Arctic Ocean, and pierced the Rocky Mountains to look on the Pacific. They came in such numbers and opened so many competing trading posts, that they almost made the trade non-viable. The solution was the gradual development of partnerships; and these, before the end of the century, had combined to become the North West Fur Company.

The Nor'Westers gradually perfected their trading and distribution system, by which they almost spanned the continent in their canoe brigades. Each summer saw the grand conclave at Fort William, named in 1807 for William McGillivray, one of three nephews of Simon McTavish, pioneer founder of the North West Company. There, the large lake canoes from Montreal would meet the smaller river canoes from the West. Furs and trade goods were exchanged. Everyone would celebrate, and the partners would plan Company policy.

We know that many of the Nor'Westers were Presbyterians, because in 1792, when St. Gabriel Street Presbyterian Church was built in Montreal, "the Subscription list for the building reads like a Who's Who of the Montreal merchants of the day, including virtually every nabob of the fur trade—Alexander Mackenzie and Simon Fraser, famous explorers of the Arctic and Pacific regions, the Forsyths, and John Richardson, whose trading company still operates in the grain and stock markets, and William McGillivray, chief director of the North West Company and opponent of Lord Selkirk's Red River Settlement, to name only the most historically outstanding contributors."[2] "The St. Gabriel Church, in the heyday of the fur trade, must have been one of the wealthiest congregations of any denomination at any period in Canadian history."[3] "As the home church of Montreal's rich fur trading community, (St. Gabriel St. Church) occasionally witnessed the baptism of children of illicit unions between traders and western "Indian" women who were recorded in the church register as "mother unknown."[4]

THE HUDSON'S BAY HIGHLANDERS

Having resolved the problems of excessive competition among themselves, these wealthy Presbyterians and others still had one effective competitor, the Hudson's Bay Company. It was the well organized and widespread competition of those who became the North West Company that forced the Hudson's Bay Company to send their Orcadians up the rivers from the posts on the shores of the Bay to meet the Indians at the points where they were being intercepted on their way to the Bay, and far beyond those points. It was noted that the Scottish Highlanders among the Nor'Westers seemed to have a greater affinity with the Indians, and greater facility with both Indian and French languages than the rather reserved Orkney men. Therefore, about 1810, the Hudson's Bay Company began to employ Highlanders also. Competition became very intense. Rival trading posts spread along the rivers far across the North and West, and even over the mountains. Thus a third group of Presbyterians appeared—the Hudson's Bay Highlanders.

CONCERN FOR THE FAITH

Many of the Hudson's Bay men became officers of the Company, and made its service their careers. Some of the Nor'Westers became "wintering partners" who spent their lives in the Northwest. While some men brought brides from Scotland or Canada, most of them tended to make permanent alliances with Indian women. These men were concerned about the education and religious training of their Halfbreed children. Most of these children grew up in isolated trading posts. Their knowledge and experience of Christianity depended on the faith of their fathers. In many cases that faith was Presbyterian.

So it was that at the beginning of the nineteenth century, along with full-blood Indians and Métis, there were hundreds of people of Presbyterian persuasion living in widely separated places across the hills and prairies of the great Northwest.

CHAPTER TWO

LORD SELKIRK AND ASSINIBOIA, 1771-1822

In 1811, the people of the fur trade in both the Hudson's Bay Company and the North West Company were thoroughly shaken. From London to York Factory; from Montreal to Fort William; and so to all the far-flung forts and posts, the disturbing word was heard. The Select Committee of the Hudson's Bay Company had sold (for a nominal sum) the whole of the Red River drainage basin to the Earl of Selkirk, for the purpose of agricultural settlement. The area, five times larger than Scotland, would be called Assiniboia. Many shareholders and servants of the Hudson's Bay Company objected to the decision, feeling that a colony would be harmful to the fur trade. To the partners of the North West Company the prospect of a colony on the Red River was threatening and completely unacceptable. In spite of the opposition, Lord Selkirk immediately began to organize a settlement.

A devastating new chapter was about to begin in the story of the Presbyterians of the Northwest. Not only were many of the fur traders and their children Presbyterians, but so were the new characters in the drama—most of the settlers, and Lord Selkirk himself.

The key figure in this new chapter was Thomas Douglas, 5th Earl of Selkirk. Thomas Douglas was born to a life of privilege, but as the seventh son of the 4th Earl of Selkirk he had no expectation, in his youth, of ever matching the privilege with power and wealth. Born in 1771, he lived through stirring times. His home was at beautiful St. Mary's Isle at the mouth of the River Dee in Kirkcudbright at the southern tip of Scotland.

When Thomas was five years old, the American War of Independence began. His father and others of the local aristocracy were at first sympathetic to the American objectives, but that changed when, in 1778, a native of the district, John Paul (who had recently taken the surname 'Jones'), joined the Americans and attacked St. Mary's Isle with an American gunboat. He probably hoped to seize the Earl, but the Earl and several of his sons were away from home. Jones contented himself with taking some of the household treasures. Seven-year-old Thomas never forgot that night. Years later he wrote:

> This was a momentous event in my life. I was terribly afraid. The firing of the cannon during the night terrified me…and when I was but a youth I developed an antipathy for the United States due almost solely to the buccaneering of John Paul.[1]

In 1786 when he was only fifteen years old, Thomas went to the University of Edinburgh, where he studied Law. Robert Burns had just published his first book of poems, and was creating excitement in Edinburgh. Adam Smith, the economist, was retired but still giving occasional lectures. Walter Scott was a friend and fellow student; Dugald Stewart was one of their teachers. Thomas was intelligent and broadly cultured, but shy and excessively modest. Although his home was far from the Highlands, he visited the glens during University holidays. There he saw the misery of the people who had been dispossessed and become redundant as a result of the Highland Clearances.[2] Thomas studied Gaelic and succeeded in mastering it, with a view to fitting himself to improve the lot of the Highland poor.[3]

The French Revolution began during Douglas's university years, and in 1790 he visited France, as did many curious British at that time. "He saw a leaderless people, (and was) alienated from the pleasing theories of optimistic popular government."[4]

In 1792 Douglas made an extensive tour of the Highlands. It became a passion with him to help his hungry and wretched countrymen. However, like other young men in his station he made the obligatory Grand Tour of Europe in 1793-4: "In Switzerland he met Count Andreani, the traveller, who was probably the first to direct Douglas's attention to the New World."[5]

The years of the 1790s were sad ones for the Douglas family. One after another of the sons died. In 1797 the sixth son died. Thomas became Lord Daer, and knew that if he survived his father, he would become the Earl. This development, which in his youth had seemed so unlikely, would give him the opportunity and ability to put his desires and dreams into action.

The only solution to the desperate situation in the Highlands seemed to be emigration. It distressed Douglas, however, to see people slipping away privately, singly or in families, mostly to the United States, mainly to the Carolinas where others had preceded them. He would have liked to see them going to British possessions, where they would not be lost to Britain; and in larger groups or extended families, so that they could help and support one another in the new life.

In 1799 his father died, and at twenty-eight years of age, Thomas became the fifth Earl of Selkirk and a member of the House of Lords. His new position with its wealth and prestige coincided with the beginning of the new century, a time of anticipation and high hopes, when everything seemed possible.

J.B. Pritchett, in his book *The Red River Valley, 1811-1849*, tells us that one of the first concerns of the new Earl was the perennial problem of Ireland.[6] There had been a revolt against British rule there in 1798, and in 1800 the imposed solution was to unite Ireland with Great Britain as part of the United Kingdom. This brought much enmity, oppression and suffering.

Extensive travel in Ireland in 1801 convinced Lord Selkirk that the solution for the Scottish problem would also be the remedy for Ireland's woes and Britain's problem. In the winter of 1801-02 he addressed a Memorial to the Colonial Office entitled "A proposal tending to the permanent security of Ireland". In it he proposed a colony in North America expressly for Irish Catholics, with assistance from the Public Purse for its establishment. He was confident that a very large number of Irishmen might be "induced" in the course of a few years, and the emigration might be so managed as to free Ireland in a relatively short time of all its most troublesome elements. The site of this Irish settlement could be Louisiana. Napoleon had recently forced Spain to cede to France New Orleans and the area west of the Mississippi. East of that was the United States. Peace negotiations were then pending between France and Britain. Lord Selkirk suggested that Louisiana might be secured for Britain. In the haste and secrecy of the peace negotiations Louisiana was not even discussed.

Coincidental to this time (1801) Sir Alexander Mackenzie published his *Voyages*, reporting on his travels in the Northwest and his discovery of the Arctic and Pacific Oceans. This book created great excitement. Lord Selkirk must have read it with mounting interest for he followed its reading with a study of all the information he could find.

At the end of March 1802 Lord Selkirk submitted to the Secretary of State a new proposal regarding Irish emigration which he called "a radical cure such as military coercion cannot effect."[7] He offered "to undertake the responsibility for the enterprise, not hesitating to devote his personal exertions and the best years of his life to the service of his country in carrying these views into execution."[8] A few days later the Earl followed this offer with a more detailed proposal addressed to Lord Hobart, the Secretary for War and the Colonies. It was in this document that Lord Selkirk first referred to the Red River. He pleaded for a colony "upon the waters which fall into Lake Winnipeg, a country as fertile and of a climate far more temperate than the shores of the Atlantic under the same parallel."[9] This was a very optimistic description. In this document he also suggested the possibility that a "concurrence of circumstances might some day lead to acquisition of territory on the Upper Mississippi."[10] It has been suggested that Lord Selkirk might have been insinuating that a good way to meet any French threat from Louisiana would be to let him (Lord Selkirk) colonize the Red River.[11]

The proposal concerning the Red River was refused by the Secretary of State, ignored by the Colonial Secretary, and opposed by Selkirk's university professor and friend Dugald Stewart, who warned that Selkirk would be accused of stimulating emigration, and urged him to stay home. In spite of these discouragements, it seems clear that by 1802, nine years before the grant of Assiniboia, Lord Selkirk had firmly in mind the idea which dominated the rest of his life—an inland settlement in British territory, offering new hope to the suffering and oppressed, relief to the Homeland, and strength to the Empire— in short, a settlement on the Red River.

THE PLANNING

"The decade 1802-1811 was spent in preliminary experiments in deflecting the current of Scottish emigration from the Carolinas to Eastern Canada."[12]

A Red River settlement might be disallowed by Government policy, but the need of the Irish was still not met, nor the bleeding away of the Highlanders stopped. Lord Selkirk, in an interview with Hobart, the Colonial Secretary, in the summer of 1802, won from him some willingness to grant a colony in Prince Edward Island. Selkirk proposed, in addition, a colony at the Falls of St. Mary (Sault Ste. Marie) in Upper Canada. He urged the need to establish a British presence at this strategic pass, across the river from the United States, as a guarantee for any future immigration to the Northwest lands. He also sought mineral rights to the surrounding area. He received approval for this plan, but was told not to try to settle the unruly Irish.

The Earl then turned his attention once again to the Highlanders. His agents signed up hundreds of settlers for both colonies, many of whom had planned to go to South Carolina. The Sault Ste. Marie project had to be given up. The expense was more than Selkirk could afford alone, and the Government refused any assistance. Most of the colonists, however, were willing to go to Prince Edward Island.

The Earl purchased large tracts of land in the eastern part of the Island, and successfully settled about eight hundred people there in the summer of 1803. They were mostly from Skye. He continued to send people there until about 1811. Some of the pioneer immigrants, however, had definitely wanted to go to Upper Canada. This desire motivated Selkirk to establish a settlement at

Lake St. Clair, which he called "Baldoon" after an estate belonging to his mother. This attempted settlement was a failure. Poor sanitation, disease epidemics, and finally depredations by Americans during the War of 1812, put an end to this project. Those who remained were dispersed to other areas of Upper Canada.

"(Lord Selkirk's) first experiences in colonization had only whetted his appetite, however, and not satisfied it, for he had not yet given up his dream of establishing a great settlement in the heart of Canada."[13] He realized that any progress in that direction would have to depend upon the cooperation of the Hudson's Bay Company.

In 1803 and 1804, Selkirk travelled extensively in the Maritimes, Upper and Lower Canada, and the north-easterly United States. In Montreal the young Scottish nobleman was welcomed by the self-made men of the fur trade. They entertained him lavishly, and proudly answered his many questions about the fur trade and the Northwest. In the United States, the Earl observed the success of the Quakers in encouraging the Iroquois towards agriculture and a settled way of life. Both of these experiences, and many others, were most helpful to him as he continued to plan for a Red River colony.

There followed three years of study of various matters pertaining to the future settlement. In 1805 Lord Selkirk published his "Observations on the present state of the Highlands of Scotland with a view of emigration."[14] In this document he expressed his conviction about the necessity of planned emigration involving large groups of people known to one another; and described in detail the planning and execution of the Prince Edward Island colony. He next addressed himself to two situations that would affect the settlement at Red River, namely the need to 'civilize' the Indians, and the fierce competition in the fur trade and its effect on the Indians.

In 1806-07 Lord Selkirk published two pamphlets in which he advanced proposals for dealing with both of the above situations, and showed how any progress in civilizing the Indians must depend upon a thorough restructuring of the fur trade. Since these ideas have been adapted in later years, and applied by both Church and Government, it will be helpful to set them out briefly here:

1. Some Indian boys should be taught the principles and practice of agriculture for a year or two. At the same time they must retain and improve their normal skills for hunting and fishing so that they will be perceived by their peers to be superior. Gradually all the men will realize that a secure sustenance is available from the earth, and that they need not be dependent on the chase. A school for this purpose should be adjacent to a fur trading post. Elderly traders who speak

both English and an Indian language could help the teacher and also recruit students. At some posts the trader was already teaching the half-blood children of Company servants. These, already bilingual, could also help their Indian cousins.

2. The wide open competition of the trading companies, instead of discouraging hunting, encourages it, and keeps the population constantly on the move. Moreover, every trader tries to outdo the other in plying the Indians with liquor, against the abuse of which they seem to have no defences, and which is destroying them.

3. There should be a definite boundary between European settlement areas and Indian lands. The Indian lands should be accessible to white men only by license. Only one fur trader or company would have a franchise, as it were, in a certain district. In this way competition would cease, and with it, the need to provide liquor. The servants of the trader, no longer needing to follow the Indians on the trap-line, could help with the teaching. Traders would then have a vested interest in conservation of the fur animals. These would increase and improve. The trader's profit would increase, and he could well afford the licence fee sufficient to pay for the teacher of the Indian school. The Indian, freed of the pressure to produce pelts, could pay attention to the soil.

This monopoly, so far from being contrary to the interests of the Indians, will be much for their advantage. Nothing, indeed, would be so much to their advantage as to be cut off from all trade whatever with the whites. Under the proposed plan the demand for furs will still continue; but instead of a keen and violent competition, it will become a regular and moderate demand, still affording them a market for the produce of the chase, but allowing them time to attend to other objects, and to improve in cultivation.[15]

Meanwhile, the wide open competition in the fur trade continued unabated. In 1807 Lord Selkirk realized that "the only feasible way of colonizing the Red River Valley was to ally himself with one of the great fur trading companies. ...The fur trade war was too fierce not to be dangerous to settlers."[16]

In 1807 Thomas Douglas married Jean Wedderburn-Colville. Her family were shareholders in the Hudson's Bay Company. The wars in Europe had cut off the market for furs. The Company was not making any profit. Its shares were available for a very low price. Lord Selkirk decided to ally himself with the Hudson's Bay Company. He, with his new in-laws and other friends, began to buy Company shares. The North West Company partners in Montreal realized that Lord Selkirk's purpose would be to sponsor emigration. In an effort to prevent this, they also began to buy Hudson's Bay Company shares, through Sir Alexander Mackenzie, then in London. This competition forced up the price and ended the buying battle. So it was that the future shape of development in the Northwest was being decided in a London boardroom, in a struggle between two groups of Presbyterians. Eventually Lord Selkirk's group owned about forty percent of the Company, enough to control its policies. Lord Selkirk commissioned reputable lawyers to investigate the legal status of the Hudson's Bay Company Charter of 1670. It was reported to be completely valid.

It was at this point, in 1811, after all his experiences, study and planning, that Lord Selkirk proposed to the Select Committee of the Hudson's Bay Company that they sell to him the huge area to be called Assiniboia, in return for ten shillings and the supply of at least two hundred servants a year to the Hudson's Bay Company, any of whom after ten years of service and wishing to remain in the country, would be given one hundred acres of land free. Lord Selkirk was to place as many settlers as possible on the land at a low price. The settlers would be given the protection of the Company.

Amid strong opposition this unlikely proposal was accepted by the Select Committee on 30 May 1811, and Lord Selkirk became the sole proprietor of an area of 116,000 square miles. This area was bounded by a line commencing at the western shore of Lake Winnipeg at 52 degrees latitude, 30 minutes north (south of Grand Rapids); west to Lake Winnipegosis, southwest to where the town of Winnipegosis now is; west again beyond the headwaters of the Assiniboine River; then south to the height of land which separates the Red and Missouri River systems; eastward along this height of land to the point west of Lake Superior where the waters begin to flow toward Lake Winnipeg; along these waters (Rainy Lake, Rainy River, Lake of the Woods and the Winnipeg River) to Lake Winnipeg; then northwest across the lake to the point of beginning.

In order to make this huge grant of land acceptable, and even palatable, to the Company, the Earl had to postpone his plan for civilizing the Indians and eliminating competition in the fur trade in favour of an aggressive and comprehensive plan of competition.

The land grant was but part of a policy designed to meet the Company's need for provisioning its lengthening trade routes, and to enable it to reach the distant Athabasca region where the North West Company had a monopoly.

The colony to be established at Red River would also provide servants born in the country, thus saving the Company the cost of transport from Scotland. The Company would have commercial advantage over its rival because of the much shorter Hudson Bay shipping route. Company servants, on retirement, could settle at the colony, and its very presence would establish the Company's title to the land. From Lord Selkirk's point of view the colonists would have a secure life, a market for their produce, and employment for their sons.

To the North West Company this plan spelled disaster. The Red River area was extremely important to them, no longer so much as a source of furs, but because it was the main source of meat for the fur brigades and many of the fur posts. Both companies maintained stations at Pembina where the Pembina River meets the Red, 60 miles south of the Assiniboine. From here the Métis buffalo hunters set out annually to follow the herds. The dried buffalo meat was pounded, mixed with berries and fat, and packed in buffalo hides. This was the famous "pemmican". A settlement at the Red River, protected by the rival company, and working for its advantage, could cut the Nor'Westers' supply route, and make their business impossible. Lord Selkirk may well have thought that the pemmican camps could continue as before, but to the North West Company the colony would always be a threat. Even if the supply lines were not cut off, the very purpose of the colony would seem to be to help the Hudson's Bay Company to compete with them vigorously, and to their disadvantage, in the Athabasca region. This was quite unacceptable. The North West Company set itself to do everything possible to oppose and prevent settlement at the Red River. W.L. Morton writes, "Seldom have the foundations of a colony been better planned, and seldom has planning been more frustrated by mischance, the shortcomings of agents, and the opposition of rivals."[17]

THE PLANTING

In anticipation of obtaining the grant of Assiniboia, Lord Selkirk had prepared detailed plans for the establishment of a settlement at the Red River. A former North West Company trader, Colin Robertson, had been appointed as adviser to the Hudson's Bay Company in London. His first advice was to employ Canadians in the fur posts. Next, he became an active recruiter of settlers. A Canadian former army captain, Miles Macdonnell, whom Lord Selkirk had met in Montreal in 1804, came to London to take charge of the initial work party that would prepare for the first settlers. Macdonnell was then appointed as the first Governor of Assiniboia, with Archibald McDonald as his Secretary. This team went into action. The opposition to their every move was vigorous.

There were delays and desertions. The North West Company agents were busy.

In spite of this, Macdonnell assembled a work party of thirty-six Scottish and Irish labourers. They sailed from Stornoway on the Isle of Skye in late July 1811, in a small ship accompanied by two others carrying staff and freight for the Hudson's Bay Company. Their route is followed today by a constant stream of people whose last glimpse of Scotland from the air is of those same Hebridean Islands. Soon they see the southern tip of Greenland, then Hudson Bay, and finally Winnipeg, about eight hours after boarding the aircraft. The Selkirk pioneers took eight weeks to reach York Factory at the mouth of the Nelson and Hayes Rivers on Hudson Bay. They had to winter in a makeshift camp near there. They lost half their number through desertion, intrigue and discipline. The remaining eighteen made four 28-foot boats, and with them covered seven hundred miles of river, portage and lake that brought them to the small Hudson's Bay Company store on the east side of the Red River opposite the mouth of the Assiniboine River. They arrived on 30 August 1812, after a thirteen month odyssey. Lord Selkirk's long-planned colony was planted. They were welcomed by the few Métis who lived beside the store, and also by the staff there, and even by the North West Company people at the new Fort Gibraltar across the river at the Forks. A few days later, in the presence of these people, with the hoisting of flags and the boom of a small cannon, Macdonnell and his eighteen young men took formal possession of Assiniboia.

The site chosen for the settlement was on the west side of the river about a mile north of the fort, at the big bend of the river which has ever since been called Point Douglas after Lord Selkirk, and extending further north along the river. This west side of the river was open prairie ready for cultivation. The east side was heavily wooded. It was the combination of open land, water and wood that had made the Red River, in Lord Selkirk's mind, the ideal site for settlement. Macdonnell named it "Colony Gardens", and on 7 October 1812, he planted some winter wheat at Point Douglas. Planned agriculture had begun.

Meanwhile in Britain, Colin Robertson and his agents had been recruiting settlers. The first of these arrived at Red River only two months after the work party. By early 1815 about one hundred and eighty people had arrived. Each family had paid ten pounds per person for transportation and provisions for one year. Each family would buy one hundred acres of land at five shillings per acre. The Hudson's Bay Company would buy or exchange all their surplus produce. In order to become established all their needs would be met. There would be a school, and a church with a Presbyterian Gaelic-speaking minister.

The settlers had survived hindering tactics in the old land, scarlet fever on shipboard, winters on the Hudson Bay shore, and the seven hundred mile arduous trek by water and portage to Red River. They had then been faced with an inability to settle, due to lack of the promised preparations, and insufficient food for winters. This had necessitated miserable winters at Pembina with the buffalo hunters. There they erected a cluster of cabins which they called "Fort Daer" (one of the titles of the Douglas family). Everyone had to make the sixty mile hike to Pembina and back. The inexperienced settlers could not have survived without the help of the Métis and of the Saulteaux Indian band of Chief Peguis. They persevered each summer in planting crops, and were finally able to spend the winter of 1814-15 at their homes.

Despite Lord Selkirk's instructions regarding caution, Governor Macdonnell had aroused the anger of the North West Company. Afraid of starvation for the colonists, Macdonnell had issued an order that, for one year, nothing but furs might be exported from the colony. Later, purely to emphasize Lord Selkirk's title to the area, he ordered everyone but the settlers and the Hudson's Bay Company people to leave.

At their annual meeting at Fort William in the summer of 1814, the angry North West Company partners made definite plans to end the existence of the colony. By cajolery, sympathy, and lavish entertainment at Fort Gibraltar during that first winter spent at Red River, Duncan Cameron, acting for the North West Company, persuaded four-fifths of the colonists to forsake the settlement in the spring, and to take the long canoe trip to various places in Upper Canada. Before they left, a force of Métis under Cuthbert Grant arrived. After an exchange of cannon fire, they succeeded in arresting Miles Macdonnell for theft of food from North West Company posts. The British Government had made Canadian Courts responsible for Justice in the Indian lands. Cameron held a Magistrate's warrant. Macdonnell was taken away by Cameron, along with the departing settlers.

Thirty-seven settlers had refused to leave the colony. They had received Cameron's assurance that they would not be molested if Macdonnell submitted to arrest. However, on June 15, four days after the large party had left, Cuthbert Grant and his band of Métis ordered everyone who remained to leave. Their gardens were trampled and their houses were burned. These last settlers and about twenty Hudson's Bay Company employees fled down the Red River in boats and across the length of Lake Winnipeg to Jack River (near the present Norway House). As far as anyone could tell, the short life of the Red River Settlement had ended. Completely discouraged, the remaining colonists hoped to be taken back home. Truth to tell, they no longer had a home anywhere.

Ironically, Cuthbert Grant, the leader of the Métis force, was the son of a Scottish North West Company partner and his Indian wife. He was one of the children who had been baptized in St. Gabriel St. Presbyterian Church in Montreal. He had returned to the West after being educated in Scotland.[18]

At this critical moment Colin Robertson arrived at the mouth of the Winnipeg River. The Hudson's Bay Company had taken his advice, and allowed him to employ Canadians. He was leading a large party of voyageurs to the Athabasca country. When he heard of the destruction of the colony, he sent the men on their way and went himself to the Forks. He was surprised to find that four Hudson's Bay Company men had hidden in a shed with a small gun. They had been able to drive away the last of the Métis. They had built a new Fort Douglas on the Point, had planted crops and gardens and had begun to rebuild houses.

Robertson went immediately to Jack River with this good news. He could encourage the small remnant of settlers with the further good news that another party of colonists was on the way, accompanied by the new Governor, Robert Semple. He also told them that Lord Selkirk himself planned to visit the next year. The thirty-seven all returned to Red River, and were able to harvest quite a good crop of grain and garden produce. They were joined in the fall of 1815 by the largest and last group of Selkirk settlers, eighty-four in number. Like most of those who had remained, the new arrivals were from the area of Kildonan in Sutherlandshire. After such an upsetting year, there was no preparation for wintering at the Forks, so it was back to Pembina once more.

Colin Robertson, an experienced trader, became alarmed at rumours that another attack on the colony was being planned for the summer of 1816. Jean-Baptiste Lagimodière, a good friend of the settlers, at Robertson's urging undertook to travel during the winter, on foot, to deliver a confidential message to Lord Selkirk in Montreal. He succeeded on reaching his goal, but bearing Lord Selkirk's message to Governor Semple on the return journey, he was captured and delivered to Fort William where he was put in jail.

Lord Selkirk, who found Canada to be hostile territory, tried in vain to arrange for a military force to be dispatched to Red River. He then employed some European soldiers, disbanded after the war of 1812-15. These men are usually called the Des Meurons, after one of their officers. The Earl managed to receive an appointment as a Justice of the Peace. By this time Miles Macdonnell had been freed of the charges brought against him. Lord Selkirk sent him, with a small party, to prepare the way for the main body. It was mid-June when the Earl and his soldiers left York (Toronto).

At that very time tensions were at the breaking point at Red River. More provisions had been taken by settlers from the North West Company posts, on order of the Governor. Colin Robertson had seized Fort Gibraltar, so that Hudson's Bay Company people now controlled all river traffic at the Forks.

The resurrection of the colony in such strength, along with the knowledge that the Hudson's Bay Company was now operating at Athabasca, created an intolerable situation for the North West Company. Métis from western posts began to gather secretly at Frog Plain just north of the colony. On 16 June 1816, one party was seen from Fort Douglas. Governor Semple and a small group of armed followers went out to warn them away. One shot was enough to start a battle. Within minutes the Governor lay dead, with nineteen of his men. Cuthbert Grant and his men took Fort Douglas and Fort Gibraltar. Once more, prisoners were taken to Fort William. Again the settlers plied the boats to Jack River, where this time they spent an uncomfortable winter. Once again the tender plant of the colony was uprooted.

Macdonnell, with his advance party, soon heard of what is called "the massacre of Seven Oaks". He hurried back to tell Selkirk, whom he met at Sault Ste. Marie. The Earl was planning to travel along the south shore of Lake Superior in order to approach the colony from the south. When he heard of the latest tragedy he tried, unsuccessfully, to lay charges against the Nor'Westers. He then sent Macdonnell and a party of the soldiers on the original route, while he and the rest of the band crossed Lake Superior and seized Fort William. He arrested North West Company partners and servants, and sent them to Toronto for trial. The Earl later commented that these actions were reckless and ill-judged. Lagimodière and other prisoners were released. However some evidence was found which connected the North West partners with the plan to wipe out the Red River settlement.

Macdonnell and his men reached Red River in January 1817, and seized Fort Douglas with no trouble during the night. Word was sent to the settlers at Jack River, and again they returned to Red River to meet Lord Selkirk and to replant their colony.

THE FIRST PRESBYTERIAN MINISTRY IN THE WEST

The arrival of the 1815 party of settlers marks the beginning of the Presbyterian Church in the North West country.

In attempting to fulfil his promise that he would provide the settlers with a Gaelic-speaking minister, Lord Selkirk had engaged the Rev. Donald Sage, son of the minister of Kildonan in Sutherlandshire, to accompany this group, although he was not yet fluent in Gaelic. Before embarkation at Helmsdale, it had been agreed between all parties that Mr Sage should remain with the group for a year:

In the meantime, one of the emigrants named James Sutherland, a pious and worthy man, who held the rank of elder in the Presbyterian Church, was appointed to marry and baptize, from which functions he was never released by the arrival of an ordained minister, in consequence of the difficulties in which the colony was placed.[19]

The first Presbyterian service in the North West was conducted by Mr Sutherland at York Factory in the fall of 1815, in the presence of the Governor-in-Chief of the Hudson's Bay Company, and of the new Governor of the colony Robert Semple and his staff. With the arrival of James Sutherland, says Alexander Ross, "the gospel was planted in Red River. It was the sunrise of Christianity in this benighted country."[20] Mr Sutherland served as a minister from 1815 to 1818. He was father and spiritual guide to the colonists, not only during the journey to Red River, but also through the first winter at Pembina, through the massacre at Seven Oaks, the escape to Jack River and winter there, the return to meet Lord Selkirk, and, as it turned out, yet another winter at Pembina. The year 1818 saw, as Mr Ross puts it, "an act of lawless violence on the part of the North West, who forcibly carried off Mr Sutherland to Canada."[21] He was never able to return. "He lived…in West Gwillimbury in Upper Canada to which many Red River settlers had previously come. He died in 1828."[22] Thus ended the first ministry of the Presbyterian Church in the North West, due to the fur trade wars between two parties, both led by Presbyterians.

"Of all men, clergymen and others, that ever entered this country," wrote Mr Ross, "none stood higher in the estimation of the settlers, both for sterling piety and Christian conduct, than Mr Sutherland."[23] To James Sutherland's early ministry among the settlers must surely be given much of the credit for that daily practice of their faith which sustained them through thirty-six years without a minister of their own persuasion.

THE FINAL PLANTING

Lord Selkirk and the soldiers arrived at Red River in July 1817. The Earl stayed until September. He re-established the settlers on their lands, and cancelled all their debts to him. Twenty-four river lots were surveyed. It is notable that Lot No. 1 was assigned to James Sutherland.[24] The Earl asked that the parish be named "Kildonan" after the home of most of the settlers, and he reiterated his promise to send a minister of their own persuasion. Lot No. 3 was set aside for a school, and Lot No. 4 for a church, where already there was a small meeting house and some burials had been made. The area along Main Street in Winnipeg, between Redwood and Machray Avenues, will locate these lots

James Marnoch

today. Lot No. 24 was just south of Kildonan Church and Cemetery.

A treaty was made between Lord Selkirk and Chief Peguis, and several other Indian Chiefs, by which land on both sides of the Red and Assiniboine Rivers, from Grand Forks to Lake Winnipeg on the Red, and west beyond Portage la Prairie on the Assiniboine, was conveyed to the Earl in exchange for two hundred pounds of tobacco per year. The land extended for two miles on each side of the rivers, and six miles in circumference at the Hudson's Bay sites at Grand Forks, Pembina and the Forks.

The Des Meurons, disbanded soldiers, were settled on Point Douglas and along the Seine River where it empties into the Red. Lagimodière was given a large tract of land on the east side of the Red. A highway crossing that land today bears his name, in commemoration of his long walk to Montreal.

The presence of Lord Selkirk, with his understanding and enthusiasm, greatly encouraged the settlers. While he was still at the settlement, the British Government intervened in the fur trade war, requiring the Canadian authorities to restore all properties to their original owners, and to assure freedom of movement to all parties. The summer of 1817 was peaceful at Red River. Lord Selkirk departed, satisfied that his colony was at last firmly planted.

For the Earl himself there was no peace. He became enmeshed in a web of charges and countercharges in the Canadian courts. These so depleted his purse, his health and his spirit that, after returning home to Scotland in 1818, he went to the south of France with hopes of restoring his health. He died there in 1820, aged 49.

Shortly before his death, in a letter to his brother-in-law concerning his wishes in regard to the colony, Lord Selkirk said: "I know of no consideration that would induce me to abandon it. I ground this resolution not only on the principle of supporting the settlers whom I have already sent to the place, but also because I consider my character at stake upon the success of the undertaking, and upon proving that it was neither a wild and visionary scheme, nor a cloak to cover sordid plans of aggression."[25] The last two clauses of this quotation appear on a memorial wall across Memorial Blvd. from the Hudson's Bay Company store in Winnipeg.

Sir Walter Scott wrote: "I never knew in my life a man of a more generous and disinterested disposition than Selkirk; or one whose talents and perseverance were better fitted to bring great and national schemes to a successful conclusion."[26]

Lord Selkirk's chief adversary, also his inspiration for a settlement at Red River and fellow Presbyterian, Sir Alexander Mackenzie, predeceased him by one month. He and other North West Company partners were also ruined financially as a result of all the troubles associated with the planting of the (mostly) Presbyterian settlement.

Taking Root

Even though the settlers had been given new courage and security by Lord Selkirk's visit and arrangements, it was already late in the year and they were not prepared for winter. In 1817 they had to take the long walk to Pembina once more. This pattern was to remain until 1822.

The year 1818 was a memorable one because of four events which affected the shape of the colonists' lives. As already mentioned, they lost the ministry of Elder Sutherland, and there was no further word of the promised Presbyterian minister; two Roman Catholic priests arrived, arranged by Lord Selkirk, to begin an endeavour to settle the volatile Métis. They were accompanied by a small party of French Canadian settlers. These, together with the disbanded soldiers (Des Meurons), began the work that developed into the Archdiocese of St. Boniface. The United States border was fixed at the 49th parallel across the West. A main reason for its not being farther north was the existence of the settlements at Red River and Pembina. An unfortunate surveying error left Pembina in the United States. That part of Assiniboia lying south of the border went to the States; and after an early and promising spring with plenty of time for the crops to ripen, a cloud of grasshoppers devoured every green blade, and left their eggs in preparation for a worse devastation in 1819.

A minister arrived in 1820, but not the one promised by Lord Selkirk. He was the Rev. John West, an Anglican clergyman sent by the Hudson's Bay Company and the Church Missionary Society in London as part of the Evangelical Movement to send missionaries to all parts of the world. Mr West came as a missionary to the Indians, and to whomever his services might be welcome.

By taking up a collection among the Hudson's Bay Company at York Factory when he arrived, Mr West began the work of the Bible Society in the North West. He continued this work at Red River. He distributed Bibles in English, Gaelic, German, Danish, Italian and French. The Bible Society is thus one of the oldest organizations in the North West.

The settlers were very disappointed that the minister was not a Presbyterian as promised. Surely Lord Selkirk's agent had betrayed the Earl's intention. They complained that "there were not twenty individuals in the whole colony belonging to the Church of England."[27] However, they worked with Mr West to build the settlement's non-Roman church in 1822, on the designated lot. It was named "St. John's". Mr West held services and also taught school there. The Presbyterians faithfully attended these services.

A few months after Lord Selkirk's death and John West's arrival, an event occurred which further shaped the settlement. The rival fur companies united in 1821 under the name of the Hudson's Bay Company. Both parties were driven to this sensible solution not only by the Red River troubles, but also by the cost of the far flung operations reaching to the Pacific Ocean. There was peace at Red River, and some growth. The process of amalgamation of the two companies resulted in the retirement of men to the settlement, with their Indian wives and half-blood children. They received pensions and grants of land. They settled mostly north of the Selkirk settlers, from Image Plain (Middlechurch) to beyond the Grand Rapids (St. Andrew's), also west along the Assiniboine (St. James). Métis hunters from Pembina joined the settlement. The latter made their headquarters in the districts now called St. Vital and St. Norbert on the Red River, and Headingley, White Horse Plain and St. François-Xavier on the Assiniboine. In this latter area lived Cuthbert Grant the former enemy of the settlement. As the acknowledged leader of the Métis he was appointed "Warden of the Plains". He was paid to defend the settlement from the war-like Sioux across the border, and also to defend the Hudson's Bay Company monopoly from the competition of the free traders south of the border. His headquarters was called "Grantown".

The administrative centre of the Hudson's Bay Company and government was established in a new fort at the Forks. It was named for the officer who had supervised the details of amalgamation of the fur companies—Nicholas Garry.

By 1825 the Red River Settlement had assumed the approximate size and shape which it was to retain for about forty-five years. Lord Selkirk's settlement had finally taken root, a small garden of civilization in the "great lone land". The Fort William–Montreal supply route was all but abandoned in favour of the shorter Hudson Bay route. As a result, communications with Canada became almost non-existent.

CHAPTER THREE

ALEXANDER ROSS AND A CONGREGATION IN WAITING, 1822-1851

COMING-TOGETHER

The Red River Settlement did not easily become a community. There were strong tensions pulling people apart. The retired Hudson's Bay Company people and the retired Nor'Westers, who had been fierce enemies in business, came to live alongside one another among the Selkirk settlers whose presence had been a major cause of their enmity. They brought their Indian wives and their half-blood children, whereas the settlers had come from Scotland as families. There was a perceptible coolness between the Orcadian and Scottish fur traders. All of them spoke English and usually an Indian language as well. The settlers loved the Gaelic. The latter were poor, thrifty, struggling farmers. The retirees had the freedom to choose between farming, trading and leisure.

THE CHURCHES

If there were tensions among the several types of British people on the west side of the Red River, there were certainly tensions also on the east side, among the Métis, the more recent French Canadian settlers, the Des Meurons and Swiss craftsmen and townspeople. The last named had been recruited by an agent of Lord Selkirk with poor judgement as to how they might fit in at a very new settlement. However, the presence of the Roman Catholic priests helped to form all of these elements into a community centred on that Church. For some of the English-speaking people on the west side of the river, notably the Orcadians, the modified Anglican services at St. John's Church were quite satisfactory. For the Selkirk settlers, and the Scottish origin families who joined them, these services could never be more than a temporary arrangement. The settlers had experienced the brief ministry of James Sutherland, which had been so suddenly ended. The young minister Donald Sage, left at home to improve his Gaelic, never arrived. There was no explanation of his absence. The Presbyterians took their stand upon Lord Selkirk's promise of a minister of their own persuasion. In 1822 they began to press for the fulfilment of that promise. Their pleas to the managers of the Selkirk estate seemed to fall on deaf ears, and the Hudson's Bay Company apparently ignored them. It was suspected that not everyone among them really wanted a Presbyterian minister. It was possible that some of their messages never saw Britain.

While waiting for a minister these Presbyterians in a strange land sang the Lord's song. Following the custom of generations, they shared family worship daily. It is a strong testimony to their faith that they did so, for it is sad to relate that too often during the Highland Clearances the ministers took the part of the landlords. The latter, of course, paid their stipends.

In their distress some of the people felt that the Lord must be justly punishing them for sins of which they were not aware. The dark sense of being deserted by the Lord was the experience of some of the men who had become the fur traders. Fortunately, the settlers from Kildonan in Sutherlandshire had a sympathetic and supportive minister in Alexander Sage, the father of the young man who had been engaged to share their new life at Red River. James Sutherland had been an elder at Kildonan, and must have influenced the people to continue their religious practice in spite of all their trials and disappointments.

THE SHORTER CATECHISM

Typically, the father led the family in prayer and praise (the Psalms in metre) at meal time. Passages from the Bible were read, explained and discussed. Then came the teaching in the form of catechizing. The father, or one of the family, asked questions from the Shorter Catechism, and the others recited the answer. The Shorter Catechism is so called because it is the shorter of the two catechisms produced by the Assembly of Divines and Members of Parliament which served as an Advisory Committee to the Parliament at Westminster in London from 1643 to 1649.[1] No wonder it has been said that Presbyterians were brought up on porridge and the Shorter Catechism. In the early days at Red River the porridge was often not to be found, but the Bible and the Catechism were open regularly. As the family gathered to receive strengthening food for the body from the wife and mother, they also received strengthening food for the soul from the husband and father. That faith which the fathers in the fur posts had tried to pass on to their children was expressed in the same terms in the homes of the Selkirk settlers. The unfamiliarity of the Anglican services was balanced for them by the familiar words of the Catechism: "Man's chief end is to glorify God…."[2] Those in the colony who shared such thoughts daily formed a community, an unorganized congregation, needing only the promised minister to become a complete Presbyterian parish. They did, however, lack strong leadership to guide and encourage them toward this goal.

THE SCOTTISH CHIEF

Out of the far West in 1825 came Alexander Ross to settle at Red River. Retired from the Hudson's Bay Company service, he was in the prime of life at age 42. His career had led him on a long journey. Born in 1793 in Nairnshire in the north east of Scotland, he had come to Canada in 1805. He taught school in the Glengarry area of Upper Canada for five years. In 1810 he joined the service of John Jacob Astor in New York, and sailed around Cape Horn to become a fur trader in the Oregon region. He had served for fifteen years in the fur trade, under Astor, the North West Company and the Hudson's Bay Company successively. He had become a Chief Trader. It is said that he turned down the offer to take charge of all the Hudson's Bay Company operations west of the Rocky Mountains. In 1813 he married Sarah, the beautiful daughter of an Okanagan Chief. By now they had three children, and his concern was for their education and religious training.

Ross decided to take his family over the mountains and across the wide plains to Red River, where there would be both school and church. The Hudson's Bay Company granted him the land upon which Miles Macdonell had built his original "Colony Gardens". The Ross home kept the name. The house stood above the river where the Point Douglas bend begins. On that land today stand the Concert Hall, the Museum, the City Hall and the Public Safety Building. Alexander, Pacific, Ross, James and William Avenues are reminders of Mr Ross, his family and his career. He became a successful farmer, and later on, a free trader, author, and Sheriff of Assiniboia. A Presbyterian, he threw in his lot with that community and quickly became their recognized leader and spokesman in their quest for a minister of their own.

Like them, too, he and his family joined in attendance at, and active support of, the Anglican services at St. John's Church. In doing so they took their part in a most curious chapter in the story of the Protestant churches in the North West—"the story of the Church of England…staying itself upon the Scottish colonists, who accorded it support while never wavering one jot or tittle from their allegiance to their own denomination."[3] At the same time, the Scots continued to petition all responsible parties to fulfil Lord Selkirk's promise of a minister of their own persuasion.

When the Anglican minister, Rev. John West, left the colony in 1823 there were high hopes that he might be succeeded by a Presbyterian. They were doomed to disappointment. West's successor was another clergyman sent by the (Anglican) Church Missionary Society, the Rev. David Jones. He soon received an assistant, the Rev. William Cockran. When Jones informed his superiors in London about "the unchristian selfishness and narrowness of mind in our Scottish population",[4] the Secretary wrote back:

> Red River is an English Colony, and there are two English mission-
> aries there already; and if the petitioners were not a set of canting
> hypocrites, they might well be satisfied with the pious clergymen they
> have got.[5]

Mr Jones actually went to considerable lengths to modify the form of service for the Presbyterians, and so maintained their presence and support at St. John's Church. With the arrival of Mr Cockran a church was built at Image Plain, and named St. Paul's. Those who built the church, and were depended upon to support it, were in fact Presbyterians. Yet Mr Cockran could write:

> I will preach them the truths of the gospel and they must listen to me;
> they have nothing to do with our forms; I will not allow them an inch
> of their will.[6]

Alexander Ross arrived at Red River as the new St. Paul's Church was about to be opened. He quickly grasped the situation, and began to articulate the cause of the Presbyterians and their long-standing expectation of a minister. Mr Cockran soon followed Mr Jones's example of the greatly modified Anglican service.

Such matters became purely academic in 1826, when the worst of the periodic Red River floods was experienced. The valley became a wide lake. Houses and barns were swept away, along with much of their contents. The people fled to higher ground around Stony Mountain on the west, and Bird's Hill on the east. The Church of St. John's was devastated. Mr Ross, accustomed to command, became a calm, much respected leader in the whole community during the crisis. Alexander Ross became "the Scottish Chief" to settlers and former fur traders alike, whose hereditary leaders had failed them and were far "over the water".

Mr Cockran organized the building of a church at Grand Rapids, and named it St. Andrew's. St. Andrew's became known as the lower church, St. Paul's as the middle church, and St. John's as the upper church. Mr Cockran planned and encouraged the settlement of the Peguis Band on the east side of the Red River north of St. Andrew's. The church built there was named St. Peter's. Along with the development of these churches, the clergy, both Anglican and Roman Catholic, opened missions to Indian people at numerous places along the water routes. Mr Ross noted that many of these missions had been closed. For years he studied the possible causes of these closures, and slowly developed his own strategy for a successful mission to Indian people. While the Anglican and Roman Catholic Churches expanded, served by clergy given every support by the Hudson's Bay Company, Ross's petitions on behalf of the Presbyterians continued to fall on deaf ears.

A NEW REGIME

In 1834 the Selkirk estate returned the grant of Assiniboia to the Hudson's Bay Company for about half the amount which had been expended upon it. The settlers were now governed directly by the Company, and this change could only be perceived as a step removed from Lord Selkirk's promise. In the next year about one hundred and fourteen persons left the settlement to travel to Iowa where they had some expectation that there was a Presbyterian church and minister.

The remaining Selkirk settlers were approached by the Governor of Assiniboia to give up the right of distilling their own liquor (thirty gallons per family, per annum, as laid down by Lord Selkirk) and allow the Company to have a monopoly. The incentive to do so was the verbal assurance of getting a Presbyterian minister. This extremely difficult sacrifice was agreed to by these Scots. When the Company's senior official in Rupert's Land, George Simpson, became directly involved with the affairs of the colony, and heard of this amazing choice, he undertook to honour the bargain and produce a minister within twelve months. Many more than twelve months went by. The monopoly was established, but the pledge was not honoured. It was noticeable that in his annual official visits to Red River, the Governor avoided the homes of the Scots.[7]

In contrast to this stagnant state of affairs, the Presbyterians at Red River were indeed surprised to learn in 1840 that Governor Simpson had agreed with the British Wesleyan Missionary Society that the Company would provide travel, room and board for missionaries at Fort Edmonton, Norway House, Rainy Lake and Moose Factory, all under the superintendence of the Rev. James Evans. At that time the Anglican missionaries were restricted in their expansion plans by a dispute in England over certain funds, but Governor Simpson himself was placing severe restrictions upon the movement of the French Roman Catholic missionaries throughout the Company's territories.[8]

THE GOVERNOR AND HIS SECRETARY

George Simpson's arms-length attitude towards the Presbyterians while deal-ing officially and favourably with the British Methodists is hard to understand, since he would have been expected to be counted among the Presbyterians himself. Born to George Simpson in 1792 at Loch Broom in Ross-shire, Scotland, he was brought up at his grandfather's Presbyterian manse. At age 17 he was taken to London to finish his education. He entered the service of the Hudson's Bay Company in 1820 in Montreal, just a year before the amalga-mation with the North West Company. That major event was marked by Simpson's appointment as Governor of the Northern Department, later known as Rupert's Land. In this prestigious and responsible position he faithfully served the interests of the Company for forty years.

In 1841 the Governor was awarded a knighthood, but it was not for anything he had done. His cousin, and secretary, Thomas Simpson, spent the years 1836-39 assisting in Sir John Franklin's project to map the elusive northwest passage. Simpson completed the channel between the mainland and Victoria Island. He went to Red River to write his report, and then sought authorization for a return trip to check some of his work. Fed up with waiting for word, he left Red River on horseback in June 1840, intending to go to New York and thence to England to press his case. His body was found on the prairie a few days later. He had died of a gunshot wound, and his journal was missing. He died without knowing that his report had created a sensation in England. He had been appointed to another Arctic expedition and had been awarded a life pension. His death was never explained. The explorer V. Stefansson has said: "The greatest single contribution of the Hudson's Bay Company to the discovery of the North West Passage was made by Thomas Simpson." The knighthood was given in 1841 to George Simpson for his cousin's achievements. In that year and the next, Sir George made a trip around the world. He published an account of it in two volumes in 1847.[9]

FORWARD IN THE FORTIES

The years following the great flood of 1826 were good years at the Red River Settlement. The cultivated land increased along the narrow lots, and livestock thrived on the pastures. The population increased slowly. Good schools trained the children well. The Red River cart brigades began to screech their way regularly to St. Paul and back with trade goods. The settlers followed the rhythm of the seasons. The pattern of the Anglican services on Sundays, with Presbyterian devotions and instruction at home, became established in the

Scottish community. After more than thirty years the hope of a minister of their own burned low.

To the south of the settlement, in the Minnesota Territory, Presbyterians were establishing missions among the Indian people. Their evangelism was not only through preaching, but also through education and, especially, agriculture. In 1843 two of the ministers journeyed down the Red River to the settlement to buy cattle. They returned the next year. When it became known that they were Presbyterian ministers, there was joy in the Scottish families. The visitors were invited to home after home for meetings. Services were held, the Word was expounded, Psalms were raised. The travellers took with them many gifts of appreciation, and they left behind them a bright flame of new hope and longing.

Alexander Ross went to work, and very quickly a new petition in his distinguished prose found its way to the Governor and Committee of the Hudson's Bay Company in London. After recounting the history of the settlement and of Lord Selkirk's repeated promise, it read:

> That the attention of your petitioners has long since been turned with painful solicitude to their spiritual want in this Settlement; that widely scattered as they are among other sections of the Christian family and among many who cannot be considered as belonging to it at all, they are in danger of forgetting what they have brought with them into this land, where they sought a home, nothing so valuable as the faith of Christ, and the primitive simplicity of their own form of worship; and that their children are in danger of losing sight of those Christian bonds of union and fellowship which characterize the sincere followers of Christ.

> That your petitioners do not deny but they have enjoyed some gospel privileges in this place, not to insinuate that the promises of Christianity belong exclusively to their Church; but rather to state that they are strongly attached to their form of worship, and wish to enjoy the freedom of serving God according to the dictates of their consciences, and the rules prescribed by their own Church, within whose bosom your petitioners have been nurtured; and believe and are persuaded that it speaks more forcibly and powerfully to their hearts than any other, and that within its pale, and within it alone, they wish to live and die.

> That your petitioners, forming as they do, one of the more orderly,

industrious, and intelligent parts of this community and feeling conscientiously devoted to their Church, can no longer abstain from appealing to the generosity and liberality of your Honourable Board in the fond hope that the prayer of their petition will not pass unregarded, and that you will not withhold from them the boon which you have afforded to other denominations of Christians in this country—that is to say, the means of spreading God's work, and fulfilling His purpose of love towards mankind, and of making Him more fully known in this land of His fallen creatures, for their adoration.

That your petitioners are mortified to see, year after year, Roman Catholic priests brought into the Settlement—at present no less than six, over a population of some 3,000—and Church of England missionaries, no fewer than four over a few; while your petitioners are left to grope in the dark, without even one. And your petitioners were the first, the only regular emigrants in the Colony, and on the faith of having a clergyman of their own Church, they left their native country.

Therefore, your petitioners would most humbly and respectfully implore your Honourable Board to send to this Colony, a Presbyterian clergy of the Kirk of Scotland, for their edification and instruction and, as their means will furnish him with but a small stipend, you would be pleased according to your usual liberality to contribute something towards his support, in like manner as you have done for all missionaries sent to your territories.[10]

This moving presentation stirred the Honourable Board only enough to send a reply. This was an encouraging advance in the minds of people whose many previous appeals had met only with silence, but the answer was "No". The Board knew of no promise made by Lord Selkirk, and no stipulation about a Presbyterian minister had been made when the Settlement was transferred to the Company. If the Presbyterians chose a minister for themselves, the Company would provide passage for him, but he would have to be supported by the people themselves. The difference between a minister for the Presbyterian congregation and the other clergy was that the latter were supported as missionaries to the Indians.

Requests were sent also to the Church of Scotland, the mother church to whom the settlers were so attached, but who never seemed to have been interested in her long departed children. The Kirk in the late 1840s was still recovering from the Disruption of 1843 and the formation of the Free Church of Scotland, and there was still no reply to the Red River Presbyterians. The appeal was sent to the Free Church.

Word came in 1849 from the Rev. John Bonar of the Free Church. They were actively searching for a minister, and expected one to be on his way very soon. The Presbyterians met to consider this new situation. Mr Ross would interview Sir George Simpson about a church building. Mr Ross laid claim to the Upper Church of St. John, built by Presbyterians on the lot given to them by Lord Selkirk. Failing agreement on that, the Anglicans could keep the building, but the Presbyterians must have the lot. Sir George's own officials at Fort Garry urged him to make a church available to the Presbyterians. The Anglican work had just been organized as the Diocese of Rupert's Land with the Rev. David Anderson as the first Bishop. He intended to make St. John's his Cathedral. There would be difficult negotiations between the Presbyterians, the Bishop and the Company. Sir George urged a favourable settlement of the problem upon his superiors in London. He was about to leave on furlough, and his place was taken by Governor Eden Colvile, who came in 1850 to reside at Lower Fort Garry.

In the end, Colvile proposed to the Governor and Committee of the Hudson's Bay Company in London that:

1. St. John's Church be valued by arbitration or otherwise and an appropriate amount be paid each seceder from the congregation.
2. The right of burial in the existing churchyard be reserved. With these two propositions the Bishop of Rupert's Land has expressed his entire concurrence.
3. A grant of Frog Plain be made to the trustees of the Presbyterian community to be held in trust for a church, a churchyard, schoolhouse, and glebe; and recommend a grant of one hundred and fifty pounds toward erection of a church.

Colvile added the comment:

I am of the opinion that they will find so much difficulty in raising a sufficient sum to build and endow a church that when the apparent grievance is done away with, in all probability the agitation of the question will cease. The Frog Plain is a very convenient locality for the purpose, in the heart of the Scotch settlement, and it is about the size of an ordinary lot of land, though from the swampy nature of the soil

I believe a very small portion of it fit for cultivation. I may mention that the individuals who think themselves aggrieved are among the most thriving and orderly of the population.

This time London answered very promptly: "Pay the 150 pounds and grant of land at Frog Plain."[10]

On 9 May 1851, Alexander Ross received the title deed to the first Presbyterian Church property in Western Canada. It was described thus:

> FROG PLAIN. Running from the west bank of the Red River N56'W one hundred and fifty four English chains or thereby, thence S56 1/2'W thirty four chains and twenty five links, from thence S56'E to the bank of the river and along the course of the same to the place of beginning. Lot 196-Series 319-1-26 F. Plain. (A chain consisted of 100 links and was 66 feet in length.)[11]

Of the four purposes for which the land was given, one had already been accomplished. In 1849 some of the settlers had organized their own school district and had built a log schoolhouse at Frog Plain.[12] In that same month of May 1851 as the property deed arrived, word came that a minister had been appointed and would soon be on his way. It thus became urgent to plan for a church building, to prepare a globe (plot of cultivated land belonging to a parish church), and to erect a manse. The last was a priority.

After much effort, Mr Bonar of the Free Church in Scotland had felt compelled to transfer the task of finding a minister for Red River to his relative and former colleague Dr Robert Burns of the Presbyterian Church in Canada (Free), the minister of Knox Presbyterian Church in Toronto. The energetic and evangelistic Burns did not rest until he had fastened on his choice. He was so certain of the outcome that he informed Mr Ross of the imminent arrival of a minister before he had actually received consent. On the strength of the message a party set out with Red River carts to meet the new minister at St. Anthony's Falls (St. Paul) five hundred miles away.

The frame of the manse was soon built. The house would serve as a meeting place until a church could be built. The faithful and articulate Alexander Ross, the "Scottish Chief", had done his work well. The thirty-nine years of the congregation-in-waiting were over. All things were now ready, a minister was coming, and they would be a Presbyterian congregation indeed.

CHAPTER FOUR

JOHN BLACK AND KILDONAN CHURCH, 1851-1870

ROBERT BURNS' CHOICE

The unsuspecting subject of all the excitement at Red River, the man whom the carts were lumbering across the plains to meet at St. Paul, was in Montreal wrestling with the problem of the direction his future ministry should take. In May of 1851 John Black had resigned as Secretary of the French Canadian Missionary Society. While still employed by the Society he had felt dissatisfied with his performance for them. He had tried for three years to improve his use of French, but had been much interrupted by the need of several English-speaking congregations of the (Free) Presbyterian Church in Lower Canada for supply preaching. The congregation at North Georgetown south of Montreal was calling him to become their minister.

"I am not resolved what I shall do", he wrote to his brother James, also a minister. "It is one of the most desirable in the Lower Province, within six hours of Montreal—considerable French population in the region of it, and this ought to weigh something with me.... I shall in all probability accept their invitation.... With faithful labour and God's blessing that field may be mostly won to our Church, and, what is better, we may hope many souls won to Christ. What shall I do? I pray that I may be directed aright."[1]

John Black's prayer "to be directed aright" was not a new one, but rather had been, and would continue to be, the hallmark of his life. Born in the Scottish Border country to shepherd folk on 8 January 1818, and brought up there among the books which the shepherds loved to read and discuss, John accompanied his parents and family when they emigrated to New York State in 1841. He was 23 years old and, after much prayer, was certain that he had a call to the ministry. When the family was settled near relatives at Bovina Centre in the Catskill Mountains, John taught school for a while to make some money. He and two cousins then enrolled in the Delhi Academy at the County town, taught by the Rev. Daniel Shepherd.

After an excellent education at Delhi, John was ready to study theology. He was in a quandary about choosing a seminary. While he had been brought up within the Kirk of Scotland, he and the family had become members of the Associate Church at Bovina Centre. Ministers of this denomination were required to sign the 200 year old Scottish Covenants against prelacy. John could not see the relevance of this in America. He thought of Princeton College, but found that he could not agree with the ambivalent view of slavery held by its sponsor, the Old School Presbyterian Church. The son of a neighbouring farmer, the Rev. James George, was a minister in Upper Canada. When he came home for a visit, he met and talked with John Black, and as a result, John decided to go to Queen's College at Kingston, of the Kirk of Scotland in Canada. This decision was made in 1844, a few months after the great disruption in Scotland which led to the formation of the Free Church. When the Synod in Canada met in 1844 the same disruption occurred. Queen's College remained with the Kirk, but Black's sympathies were with the new Presbyterian Church of Canada, the Free Church. As a result, when the Free Church opened a college in Toronto in the Fall of 1844, John Black was one of the fourteen students. They studied at the large table in the Rev. Henry Esson's house, using his own books, while he taught them in Arts subjects, and the Rev. Andrew King taught Theology. This was how Knox College began, and how John Black was directed to it.

The small group of teachers and students became close friends. They were very missionary minded, and soon formed the Knox College Missionary Society. They helped in city missions, heard speakers, contributed to the support of an overseas missionary of the Scottish Free Church, and served on home mission fields in the summers. When a Swiss minister spoke to them about the French Canadian Missionary Society, they became enthusiastic and sacrificial supporters of that work. They sent John Black, their only French speaker, to the Society's school at Pointe-aux-Trembles near Montreal. This exposure to the work of French evangelism led John Black to postpone his ordination to the ministry and to join the staff of the Society in 1848. He soon became their Secretary, and was at the heart of the work.

To Dr Robert Burns it must have been clear that here was the very man for Red River, an unordained Knox College graduate with experience in evangelism and a fine gift for preaching. He would send Black to Red River on an exploratory visit. Burns had joined the faculty of Knox before Black had left, so he knew his man well. To John Black, however, the picture was not so clear. He was trying to decide between French evangelism and an English parish. Red River was so far away and his aged parents were now alone. He turned down the invitation. But this was indeed the answer to John Black's prayer to be "directed aright". By the end of July he had worked through the problem and agreed that he must go. It would only be for an exploratory visit after all. Dr Burns had been right. This was the man.

John Black was ordained as a minister in Knox Presbyterian Church, Toronto, on 31 July 1851. The sermon was preached by his College friend (and later colleague) the Rev. James Nisbet. John Black was then enrolled as a Foreign Missionary of the Synod of the Presbyterian Church of Canada (Free), appointed to Red River in the Hudson's Bay Territory.

The newly ordained minister began his long journey to his people early the next morning, unaware that the welcoming party of Red River men waiting for him at the Falls of St. Anthony (St. Paul) decided on that same day that they could wait no longer. They had about a month of hard travel ahead of them, and it would soon be harvest time. They could not know that the long awaited minister was at last on his way.

An Exploratory Visit

By horseback, by lake boat, by railway, stage coach and river boat, for two weeks John Black travelled quite comfortably to St. Anthony's Falls on the Mississippi River, only to discover that his expected escort had departed. He had reached the end of scheduled transportation. How would he cover the remaining 500 miles and more?

Alexander Ramsey, Governor of the new Territory of Minnesota, was preparing to leave for Pembina near the border, in order to sign a Treaty with the Chippewas. Including staff, wagoners, and a military escort, there would be a party of about fifty men. The minister could come along at his own expense. John bought a horse and camping outfit. Twenty-five days later the party arrived at Pembina, where on the next Sunday John Black conducted his first service as an ordained minister. It was to about fifteen people, gathered with the Governor in the house of Norman Kittson. Kittson was an American fur trader whose presence at Pembina had brought much aggravation to the Hudson's Bay Company and considerable income to adventurous young men of Red River.

While at Pembina John Black met James Tanner, a Métis, who was hired as interpreter to the Governor. Black was immediately attracted to him. A man named Joe Coalier drew Black's interest to Tanner by describing him as a thoroughly converted former dangerous drunkard, who was now an able teacher of the Bible, and whose prayers were most forcible. He was married and had a family. He had served an apprenticeship with the Oberlin Presbyterian missionaries in Minnesota. They had visited Red River and were the indirect cause of Black's appointment there. Tanner was hoping to establish a Presbyterian mission farther west in the North Dakota Territory. The two became friends.[2]

The last stage of the journey was down the serpentine bends of the Red River in a birch bark canoe, accompanied by two Métis boatmen and the Governor's secretary, the St. Paul journalist, J.W. Bond, who had become a good friend of the young minister over the past weeks. Bond describes the scene that met their eyes when, after two days, they reached the Red River settlement:

> A village of farmhouses, with barns, stables, hay, wheat, and barley-stacks, with small cultivated fields or lots, well fenced, (is) stretched along the meandering river, while the prairies far off to the horizon are covered over with herds of cattle, horses, etc., the fields filled with a busy throng of whites, Halfbreeds and Indians—men, squaws, and children—all reaping, binding, and stacking the golden grain; while hundreds of carts, with a single horse or ox, harnessed in their shafts, are brought in requisition to carry it to the well-stored barn, and are seen moving, with their immense loads rolling along like huge stacks, in all directions. Add to this the numerous windmills, some in motion whirling around their giant arms, while others motionless are waiting for "a grist". Just above, Fort Garry sits in the angle at the junction of the Assiniboine and Red rivers, with a blood-red flag inscribed with the letters H.B.Co., floating gaily in the breeze. Opposite is the catholic cathedral, built of stone in 1832, and still unfinished. The bare, rough, unplastered wall, in front, is cracked and shattered, and is surmounted by two steeples; one finished and containing a chime of bells; the bare timbers of the other tower aloft, dark with age and nakedness.[3]

Such was John Black's overview of the site of his new ministry. He would soon learn of the census of 1849. There were then "2,180 Protestants (of whom some 300 may be estimated to have been Kildonan Scots and Selkirk settlers with their children), and 2,511 Roman Catholics of European or mixed blood, 460 Swampy Crees at St. Peter's, 77 Saulteaux west on the Assiniboine, and 163 military pensioners and their dependents, making a total of 5,391. There were 4 Protestant churches and 3 Roman Catholic, with 9 and 3 schools respectively."[4]

Alexander Ross was at the river bank to welcome the minister and his companion to Colony Gardens. It was the evening of Friday, 19 September 1851. In the stone house and among the Ross family the Rev. Mr Black was to make his home. He had been physically approaching it for fifty days. His people had been watching for him for thirty-nine years.

A Congregation Takes Shape

The new Presbyterian minister attended worship at St. John's Church on his first Sunday at Red River, but one week later, on 28 September 1851, three hundred people gathered with him at the uncompleted manse at Frog Plain for the first service ever held by a Presbyterian minister west of the Great Lakes. It is not given to many "foreign" missionaries to be greeted by such a congregation. They heard a sermon on the text "Unto me, who am less than the least of all saints, is this grace given, that I should preach among the Gentiles the unsearchable riches of Christ". (Ephesians 3:8)

During the following weeks, as the minister went among the people, he received into membership in full communion forty-five of them. They then elected six elders, of whom five agreed to serve. On December 7 the elders were ordained—James Fraser, Donald Matheson, George Munro, Alexander Ross and John Sutherland. With the Kirk Session constituted, the Sacrament of Baptism was observed for the first time, for the child of Richard Salter, the only Englishman in the congregation. The Session then moved toward the highlight of worship in the Presbyterian Church, Holy Communion. A preparatory service was held on Saturday, and tokens of admission were distributed. At the Communion service on Sunday, 14 December 1851, the communicants sat at a linen-covered table in relays. Mr Black wrote of this service:

> It was to all of us a solemn day, being the first time in which, according to our simple and scriptural form, that blessed ordinance was ever dispensed here. It was also the first time for the pastor who administered; the first time for the elders who served; and the first time for not a few who sat at the table—among others, two old men—the one 87 and the other 99 years of age; and all this in addition to its own intrinsic solemnity.[5]

The Council of Assiniboia had already declared all marriages, baptisms, and burials registered by a Presbyterian minister to be legal.

On the day after the first communion service, the Recorder of Rupert's Land, Adam Thom, wrote to Sir George Simpson:

> The Rev. Mr Black is a man of strong intellect and earnest utterance. You cannot listen to him without feeling his power and listen to him

you must, whether you will or not—novelties (are not they?) in Red River church-going. Nor is he less decidedly superior to his rivals in charity than in ability. Uninfluenced by the example of those, who had made a standing text of him and his people before his arrival, he has never, as I am assured, made any allusion whatever to any other denomination beyond praying every Sunday for the success of all missionaries of the gospel. Moreover this liberality of feeling does not, as is too often the case, arise from any want of zeal. To say nothing of his purely professional labours, he devotes the little leisure, which he leaves to himself, to the superintendence of the school, and that, for the first time in this place, with a view to the permanent improvement of education. As a proof that his work is appreciated, his people, burdened as they are, with the erection of a Kirk and a manse and with the maintenance of a minister and unaided by any portion of the municipal grant, have just now contributed money enough to supply their school with a complete outfit of maps and prints and books....[6]

John Black's own description of those busy early days is from a letter he wrote on 17 December 1851:

The temporary church will accommodate 250 or 300 persons, and is always well filled with a most attentive auditory. We have service forenoon and afternoon, and also a lecture on Wednesday. We have a large and interesting Sabbath-school. There are ninety-six scholars, thirty-six of whom are young people in my own class. Finding, as I did, that the congregation was pretty ripe for organization, I proceeded, with the help of a few of the heads of families, whom the people at my request appointed to aid me in my work, to examine and admit to the privilege of Church membership, such as presented themselves with this desire.[7]

The attitude of charity towards others, which Adam Thom noted in John Black, was expressed by the people at the same season. They heard of the need for food at two Anglican Missions, whose missionaries they knew well— Abraham Cowley at Fairford in the Interlake area, and James Hunter at The Pas. From their scanty stores the Kildonan folk sent to each 20 cwt of grain, along with a letter in Alexander Ross's unmistakable style:

Our offering, humble and scanty as other claims have made it will at least show that we acknowledge, if we cannot discharge, the debt which we owe to the Church Missionary Society. Though, after the struggles of more than 30 years and at an expense which attests our sincerity, we have at last established in this wilderness the faith of our fathers, yet we embrace this, the first opportunity of evincing that Christian charity which, amid the manifold divisions of the Christian church, can still knit together honest differences of opinion with a bond of mutual goodwill.[8]

In this way, in the earliest months of John Black's "exploratory visit", Kildonan, the first Presbyterian Church west of the Great Lakes, entered its organized existence—with Minister, Elders, Members, the Word and Sacraments, Sabbath-school, Day-school, and a clear witness of correspondence with other churches.

THE CHURCH BUILDING

Governor Eden Colvile's opinion of the Presbyterians' ability to build and endow a church was proven to be wrong. In the early months of 1851, long before John Black arrived, they had agreed to build a manse immediately, 35 ft by 20 ft; and to begin the building of a stone church, 60 ft by 32 ft, as soon as five hundred pounds had been subscribed in addition to the one hundred and fifty pounds from the Company.[9] "With great energy," says W.L. Morton, "they then proceeded to raise the rest of the money for building—some six hundred pounds."[10]

Limestone was quarried at Stony Mountain, several miles west of Frog Plain, and taken across the prairie by stoneboat or Red River cart. Lime was burnt at the site; timbers were brought from Bird's Hill and St. Peter's on the east side of the river, and by the end of 1851 most of the material for the church was ready for building in the spring.

The spring of 1852 was featured by the most devastating Red River flood since 1826. Because of all the destruction and disruption in the wake of the flood, it was midsummer before the building was begun. The cornerstone was laid by Adam Thom on 11 August 1852. A sealed bottle was placed within containing the names of the officers of the Church and statistical information about the Colony. Mr Ross prepared a record of the struggle to get the Church established.

The building of the stone structure was under the direction of Duncan McRae, who had behind him the building of both Upper and Lower Fort Garry, St. Andrew's, St. John's and St. Peter's Churches, as well as other Red River stone buildings. "There keep pouther an' ill hauns off her," he is reputed to have said, "and she'll staun for a hunner years an' mair." He built the foundations four feet deep, and both they and the walls are four feet thick. The design of the church was strongly influenced by the memory of the old Church of Kildonan in Sutherlandshire, but the new Kildonan was given a distinctive belfry.

William Ross, Alexander's eldest son, described the progress of the building in early November 1853:

> Our church is shingled and the spire and bell are up—the flooring in—the pulpit finished—the windows all in—one coat of plaster inside, and in a few days the ceiling will also be in.[11]

On 5 January 1854, the church was officially opened, free of debt, its total cost being one thousand and fifty pounds. John Black preached on the text Haggai 2:9, "The glory of this latter house shall be greater than of the former, saith the Lord of Hosts, and in this place will I give peace."

By the end of January, William Ross tells us, the pews had been distributed "amicably and with great cordiality".[12] This refers to the method of supporting a church which was usual among British people. The head of a family "bought" or leased a pew annually, and received a certificate which could not be transferred to anyone but a member of that church. In the case of Kildonan, each family paid two pounds, thirteen shillings, of which two pounds, ten shillings, was for the minister's stipend, and the three shillings for the support of the Precentor and the Beadle. The Precentor "lined" the Psalms and raised the tune with the aid of a tuning fork. The Beadle was the custodian and caretaker. At the time of the opening, the minister's stipend was one hundred pounds plus fifty pounds from the Hudson's Bay Company. The precentor, John Fraser, who was also foreman of the building operations, received three pounds. The beadle, Alexander Bannerman, received five pounds. The pews were drawn by lot. They could seat five hundred and ten people.

The pulpit was high against the front wall, with the precentor's desk below it. There were six box pews, square, with doors and tables, at the right and left front. Short pews marched alongside each wall, while the centre was filled with long pews. On the west side the pews reached to the back wall. In the centre there was a space in front of the door for two stoves, and on the east side, beneath a stair to the gallery, was a tiny vestry for the minister.[13]

John Black describes the scene on 31 May 1854:

> The Church building is not quite finished yet. All the pews on the ground floor are finished.... The pulpit (hexagonal) is also finished

and trimmed with blue and orange.... There are six square seats—Robert McBeath occupies that in the north west corner, and next to him, Donald Bannerman—while (Alex. Ross) and William occupy corresponding positions on the opposite side. That to the right of the pulpit (that is, when you are in it) is set apart for the Hon. H.B.C., while Mrs Black occupies that on the left side in solitary dignity. A very handsome cornice has been put round the whole, and today Hugh Matheson, John Fraser and young John Flett are busy—the former building the stair which he has more than half finished, the latter two at the front of the gallery....[14]

THE EXPLORATORY VISIT EXTENDED AND ENDED

When John Black left Toronto in August 1851, he intended to return in the spring of 1852. Several experiences conspired to postpone his departure from Red River. The first of these was the flood of 1852. His people suffered such devastation to their homes and to their spirits that he wished to be with them. The experience of sharing with them the days at Stony Mountain had forged a bond of genuine fondness between them. He conducted the Sabbath services in the open air, assuring them "that all things work together for good to them that love God, to them that are the called according to His purpose."

One of the first things that John Black, the former school teacher with such a love of learning, did at Kildonan was to become acquainted with the Kildonan school, housed in a log building on what had since become the church property. The teacher was a young Kildonan man, Alexander Matheson. John remembered his own childhood days in the Gair school near his home in the Scottish Border country, and the rich education he had received, not only in basics, but also in Bible and Literature, Latin and French. He determined to do all that he could to help the teacher and to make Kildonan the finest school at Red River. He must remain long enough to make a meaningful contribution among some of the older pupils.

In the spring of 1852, the new minister of Kildonan was invited to meet with some of the people who lived down the river, north of St. Andrew's Church at the Rapids, and south of Lower Fort Garry. Some of the retired officers and servants of the Hudson's Bay Company who had settled there beginning about 1825, with their Indian wives and Halfbreed children, wished to have Presbyterian services. They were of fourteen interrelated families and their leader and spokesman was Donald Gunn.

After serving the Company for ten years in the James Bay area, Donald Gunn retired and made his home on the west side of the river, while his son lived on the east side. The family had first settled there in 1823. Mr Gunn was a keen student, interested among other things in botany and the weather. He was for many years a regular correspondent of the Smithsonian Institute, as well as the teacher of the settlement's school.

When John Black agreed to their request for a Kirk he began to meet with them every second Sunday, staying overnight at the Gunn home. The people speedily built a log meeting house which was ready for use in the fall of 1852. This was the beginning of the congregation called Little Britain, the first Presbyterian Church Extension in the North West.[15]

At this time John Black welcomed a visit from his friend James Tanner, still seeking approval for his hoped-for mission. After hearing Tanner preach at Kildonan, and also at St. Peter's Church down the river, both Black and the Anglican rector urged the Assiniboine River area as the site for Tanner's mission. The Governor, Eden Colvile, turned down this request. Tanner did establish a mission in the North Dakota Territory. It later had to be abandoned because of murderous raids by the Sioux. Tanner's brother was a powerful chief among the Saulteaux along the Assiniboine, and Tanner did actually, though unofficially, become the first Presbyterian missionary in Western Canada—an itinerant, unpaid evangelist.[16]

Thus, a deepening pastoral relationship with the Kildonan people, a challenging educational situation, and the opportunity for church extension kept the "visiting" minister much longer than he had planned.

On the other hand, John Black had a strong desire for more study, and perhaps a scholarly ministry in the East. He was the first, but far from the last, young Presbyterian minister appointed to the West who questioned whether "Providence" (as Black always put it) really intended him to stay there very long. He would return to the East to report on his exploratory visit, and to try to resolve the direction his ministry should take, as well as to visit his parents, relatives and friends, as soon as he could arrange it. He also sincerely questioned whether he was the best choice to serve the Kildonan people. He was very conscious of his lack of the Gaelic, which the people spoke and had expected in their minister.

When the congregation called him to be their minister in the spring of 1853, John Black felt that he could not in good conscience accept. He began the long journey to Toronto in May, but he did not go alone. The first fruits of his labour and concern were the three young men who accompanied him— the school teacher Alexander Matheson, Donald Fraser, both of whom were to prepare for the ministry at Knox College, and young James Ross, the son of Alexander, who was to enroll at the University of Toronto.

RETURN AND MARRIAGE

William Ross's description of progress on the church building as of 4 November 1853 was written to his brother James at Toronto, when John Black had been absent from Kildonan for almost six months. "The season is very far advanced," he wrote, "and we have well nigh given up all hopes of his (Mr Black's) return to us this autumn.... We will certainly pass a dreary winter if none will come." Then, after detailing the state of the work at the church, he comments:

> You see we have been working—but sadly do we want him who would give fresh courage and energy to all our undertakings.... Tell old Dr Burns he has broke his pledge...and we do not thank him for it. He has not only deprived us of our minister, but also his salary which was guaranteed by the HBC to Rev. John Black and to no other.[17]

Ten days after the writing of that letter of angry disappointment, John Black walked into a warm welcome at the Ross home.

Robert Burns, on hearing of all that had been accomplished at Red River, urged John to return. He had made some attempt to secure a Gaelic-speaking minister, but without success. Correspondence from Red River was unanimous in pressing for his return. Sir George Simpson himself had proposed fifty pounds stipend from the Company if Mr Black would return.

Not without some misgivings, John Black accepted another appointment to Red River, having satisfied himself that Providence was pointing him that way, and that therefore his duty was clear, at least for some time. The journey required eight weeks. Due to the lateness of the season he had been delayed by ice forming on the rivers in northern Minnesota. He had been welcomed by the Presbyterian missionaries at Red Lake, who had held the meetings at Red River. This gave him the opportunity to observe the success of their methods of teaching agriculture and associated crafts, along with Christian education, to the Indians.

It quickly became clear that John Black's second appearance at Red River was not altogether unwilling. He became engaged to marry Henrietta, Alexander Ross's attractive daughter. Events occurred rapidly in the next few weeks. They were married at Colony Gardens by the veteran Anglican missionary, the Rev. William Cochran, on 21 December 1853. The opening of the church followed on 5 January 1854. This in turn allowed the manse to be partitioned, and the well-used structure became a residence for the first time when the minister brought his bride to it a week later.

The minister's marriage and settlement in the manse completed the establishment of the Presbyterian Church on the model of a Scottish parish, to the great satisfaction of the Selkirk settlers and the retired Scottish fur traders. The marriage also related John Black to the several members of the Ross family, and through them to others in the English-speaking Halfbreed community. This had some importance in view of the class structure which had developed in the colony. The retired Company officers were of the "upper" class, but their Halfbreed children were not. Alexander Ross had, in 1849, complained to the Governor that "the young men of mixed blood were troublesome because, though educated, they had been given no place in the upper class; they therefore sank into the lower class and led it."[18] By the time of John Black's first appearance at Red River, there had been some improvement in that situation. Some Métis and other Halfbreed men had been appointed to the Council of Assiniboia, and because the Company was unable to prevent a certain amount of free trade in furs, a number of the young men had the opportunity of a rewarding occupation. William Ross, Alexander's Halfbreed son, had recently succeeded his father as Sheriff of the Colony. The entrance of the Presbyterian minister into the Ross family caused some additional blurring of the former rigid lines.

The second extension of Presbyterian ministry at Red River was directly occasioned by Black's relationship to the Ross family. Two of the daughters were married to Halfbreed farmers in the area of Headingley on the Assiniboine. Regular services were soon being held in their homes for them and their neighbours.

HIGHER EDUCATION

John and Henrietta Black were scarcely settled in the manse when there was an unexpected change in the pattern of higher education in the Colony. Bishop Anderson of the Anglican Church was serving as Principal of the Red River Academy. He had changed its name to St. John's College. Early in 1854, for whatever reason, the Bishop announced that Presbyterian students would no longer be admitted to the College. Black's response to this development was to begin long-range plans for a Presbyterian college. He began to move toward this goal by beginning a class in Latin with four young men, and by beginning to assemble a library.[19] Throughout his ministry Black continued to teach various subjects at the high school or college level. This small beginning and continued concern for the young people eventually developed into Manitoba College.

THE MINISTER AND THE CONGREGATION

The Presbyterian habit of wishing to "do all things decently and in order" was exemplified by their first minister in the West. He planned to spend four hours per day for four days per week on systematic study: Hebrew, Greek, Theology and Bible Interpretation were the regular subjects. Added to them was a wide variety of other reading. The same four hours on the other two days were given to sermon preparation. Black's sermons were mainly textual and expository. He made good use of his hearers' knowledge of Scripture and the Shorter Catechism. "How we remember the spiritual power of the man—the intense fervour of his pulpit ministrations—the fire that made his voice ring through the church with appeals on behalf of Christ," said one who often heard him. During the service John Black, the Pastor, would announce in which of the river-front homes he would visit in the coming week. Each visit was a special occasion for both the minister and the whole family, who would all be sure to be at home.[20]

The manse was soon the home of a growing family, yet it was also the centre of hospitality and warm friendship not restricted to the Kildonan people. Black maintained a correspondence with many fur traders in their lonely posts. Often, when one of them was at Fort Garry on business, he would walk the five miles to the Kildonan Manse to visit the minister, the only one of his church in the wide land of furs. It was in recognition of this ministry that Governor Dallas requested Presbyterian services at Fort Garry. Over the years, as others besides Company staff attended, these services developed into Knox Church, the first Presbyterian congregation in the new village of Winnipeg.

John Black was able to organize interchurch prayer meetings with the several Anglican clergy. He began a Temperance League, the members of which pledged to abstain from alcohol, and he fought a constant battle against the prevalent foul language. In spite of such signs of an effective ministry, Black continued to feel dissatisfied with the spiritual results. He saw his people as too satisfied with things as they were. This was understandable among these people who had had so little, and had yearned for the time which had now come. Yet he longed for the signs of spiritual awakening and "showers of blessing". After hearing of a revival at Norway House under the Wesleyan ministry of Rev. George McDougall, Black wrote to his brother (also a minister):

> I expect if ever a revival breaks out in this country it will be among the despised Indians, or Episcopal Halfbreeds to rebuke us spiritually proud self righteous Scotch Presbyterians.[21]

Black tended to blame himself for this unhappy situation, as he wrote to James Ross:

> Our meetings and schools are on the increase—but not many tokens of spiritual life—I beseech you do not speak of my success here—(as you do in your last to your father) it sounds like mocking.[22]

Black often expressed in letters the desire to leave Kildonan for some church in the East, but when serious efforts were made in 1854 to call him to Hamilton, and to find a replacement for Red River, he wrote:

> The people here are in great consternation about it. Whether to wish that a man may be found or not, I cannot tell. Many things draw me homewards yet I am well here and the people most kind and agreeable and we have become attached to one another exceedingly. Still, if one is sent in whom I have confidence, I think I shall be able to leave with some degree of comfort.... I do not like taking one from Canada— this is making one hole to fill another. I shall wait the leadings of Providence in the matter.[23]

In 1856 here occurred two deaths in the Ross family, first the son William, and then the father Alexander. In reporting to his brother the death of his "dear and worthy Father-in-law", Black said:

> ...again it has pleased an all-wise Providence to visit us with a severe and trying affliction...the family...are left desolate.... The congregation and Session will also feel the loss exceedingly.... This appears to me a call in Providence which I must listen to. If the Church, however, insists on my leaving I shall interpret that as the voice of God and do so.... As, however, Providence has twice sent me here contrary to my own expectations and now prevents me leaving in the same way, it looks as if it may be I have to stay here and if it is clearly God's will so be it.[24]

In this spirit of self-deprecation yet commitment, of personal dissatisfaction and pastoral concern, John Black walked with his wife's family and his flock in an ever deepening bond, but without a Presbyterian ministerial colleague for over eight years (1854-1862). He longed for the Church to show a motherly care over her distant children, and send a minister to visit, so that they might hear a different voice and be encouraged; or even send a pastoral letter to be read to them.

Two events, one educational and the other personal, lifted the lonely pioneer's spirits. In response to his appeal to his former Professor, Henry Esson, he received three or four hundred books for the library in 1856. In 1859 the arrival of the first river steamboat, the *Anson Northup*, down the Red River from the south, and of a minister, Mr McTavish, to relieve him, gave him the opportunity to take Mrs Black and some of his in-laws to meet his family and friends in Canada and New York State.

Kildonan congregation extended a Call to John Black for the second time just prior to the eastern visit. He decided to accept on his return, when Mr McTavish could induct him. Unfortunately they passed each other on the return trips. Black was still a missionary.

In 1861 in Canada, the Presbyterian Church (Free) amalgamated with the United Presbyterian Church to form the Canada Presbyterian Church. John Black described the union as "a measure at once so Christlike and of so much practical consequence."[25]

A union of a different kind was in the air at Red River in 1857—union with Canada. A petition, signed by 575 people, was sent to Toronto. It was a protest against the Hudson's Bay Company's continued restrictive rule, and was accompanied by a well-written document describing the advantages of Red River to Canada. The author of this document was Donald Gunn, the leading elder at Little Britain. Thirteen changed-filled years would pass before this union was accomplished. John Black took no public stand on this or other political matters. Privately, he questioned whether such a union would bring much improvement, but thought it might reduce the sense of isolation, and might encourage the Church in Canada to engage in a Presbyterian mission among the Indians.

CHAPTER FIVE

A PRESBYTERIAN MISSION AMONG THE INDIANS

John Black had brought with him to Red River the Church's concern, not only for the settlers, but also for the Indians.[1] He learned of the kindness to the settlers shown by Peguis and his band of Saulteaux in the difficult early days; and that they, together with some Swampy Crees, were settled at St. Peter's under the guidance of the Anglican missionary William Cochran. The latter was both pastor and farm instructor to them. There was another small settlement of Saulteaux along the Assiniboine at Baie St. Paul, under the guidance of Father Belcourt. Other than these, there were no Indians living near the Red River. There were Ojibwa to the east, Sioux to the south west, Assiniboins and Crees to the far west, and Crees and Ojibwa to the north. Black learned from Alexander Ross that missionaries of the Roman Catholic, Anglican, or Wesleyan Churches had reached many of these, and that there were Catholic missions as far away as the Athabasca country. However, the nomadic, buffalo-hunting Crees of the western plains had only seen missionaries passing through their lands.

In preparation for his book *The Red River Settlement*, Ross had listed the large number of missions which, over the years, had been closed. He was critical of the missionaries in this regard, feeling that there were too many of them spending time at the settlement. The company had informed him that they supported the missionaries because of their work with the Indians. Ross had become convinced, though, that the failure of some of the missions was due to the unseemly competition of the Anglicans, the Catholics and the Wesleyans. Too often where one had gone another had followed. The Indians had responded in the same way as they did to competing fur traders. They went where the most desirable gifts were offered.

A second and more fundamental reason for the failure of missions, Alexander Ross believed, had to do with the methods employed in conducting them. His views are so similar to those of Lord Selkirk in the two pamphlets on

57

the civilization and improvement of the Indians, published in 1806-07, that it can be assumed that he somehow had access to them.

Lord Selkirk had noted two causes for the failure of attempts to instruct and civilize "savages". The first of these was "the attempt to inculcate religious and moral instruction without a sufficient basis of the habits of civilization". When some tribes had been persuaded to adopt the Christian religion by this method, they had always relapsed when the care of the missionaries was relaxed or withdrawn. The other cause of failure, when attention *had* been paid to introducing the improvements of civilized life, as well as the light of religion, was the attempt to do too much at once—"to convert a set of complete savages immediately into a civilized society". When Indian children had been removed from their parents and given a European education, on their return they had either reverted to their former ways, or they had remained with Europeans, thus in no way helping the improvement of their people.[2]

Ross had seen evidence of the first of these causes of failure in the case of the Baie St. Paul Mission. He saw another kind of failure in "too much too soon" at St. Peter's, where farm work was done only when the missionary was not only watching, but also doing it—a poor use of a minister's time, but appropriate for an experienced farmer.

Lord Selkirk's plan—a school to encourage step-by-step adoption of land cultivation by a whole Indian community—had been drawn from successful efforts by Moravians and Quakers among Indians in the United States.[3] Alexander Ross asserted that Lord Selkirk's primary object (in planting the settlement) was the spread of the Gospel, and the evangelization of the heathen.[4] Ross's own plan, therefore, was for a successful mission, and was drawn from Lord Selkirk. In it missionaries would not be directly involved during the "civilization" phase. This would be in the charge of competent farmers, and should last for several years. For "nothing by the postponement of spiritual instruction", said Ross:

>...till the heathen are in great measure independent of temporal aid can ever enable merely human eyes to form a correct view of the religious state of aboriginal converts. When a savage is offered at once food and truth—both or neither—he is at least as ready as civilized men, whether laity or clergy, to take the one for the sake of the other; in fact he is strongly tempted to consider what he calls 'praying' as something that makes the pot boil.... Though Christianity be the end, yet civilization is nevertheless the best means—not only the best means of introducing that end, but, still more dearly, the sole means of enabling it, when once introduced, to perpetuate itself.[5]

John Black absorbed all of this knowledge and theoretical planning. When he returned to Red River in 1853 he was inspired by all that he had heard and seen of the successful application of very similar ideas by the Oberlin group of Presbyterian missionaries among the Chippewa of Northern Minnesota. He had ample opportunity of discussing the whole subject with his father-in-law, and probably of influencing the final script of Mr Ross's *The Red River Settlement*, which was published in 1856. The Scottish Chief died later in that same year, aged 74. John Black became not only the executor of his estate, but the custodian of his ideas about a mission to the Indians.

To Lord Selkirk at the beginning of the century, the civilization of the Indians was a necessity because of the deterioration of game as the result of the excessive demands of competitive fur traders, and the thirst of the Indians for the liquor they offered. As John Black considered the matter half a century later, he would be aware of the reports of the extensive study of the prairies by both the Palliser group from Britain and the Hind group from Canada, with their encouragement toward immigration. For the Indians, the uncertain life of dependence on the chase would become ever more difficult, as settlement drove the game animals farther and farther away. In addition to his constant concern for evangelism, Black felt it to be urgent that the nomadic Cree hunters of the western plains learn to till the soil.

John Black found it embarrassing and wrong that of the four churches established in the West, the Presbyterian was the only one with no work among the Indians. He also found himself reluctant to urge his people to pray for and support distant Presbyterian missions while their Church provided them no avenue for meeting the crying need near by.

With a concern for the evangelization of the Plains Cree, and with a plan which would be of much value to them daily; with a regard to the needs of his congregations for missionary involvement, and wishing his denomination not to fall behind others in outreach, Black persistently, year after year, pleaded with the Foreign Mission Board to institute a mission. There were good intentions but no action, until after the formation of the Canada Presbyterian Church in 1861. Possibly the additional resources enabled the Church to respond in a tentative way in 1862, by appointing a minister to assist John Black at Red River and to help prepare the way for a mission to the Indians.

JAMES NISBET

The second Presbyterian minister appointed to serve in the Hudson's Bay Territories was the Rev. James Nisbet, the former classmate of John Black at Knox College. When he had preached the sermon at Black's ordination on 31

July 1851, Nisbet had been the minister of Knox Presbyterian Church, Oakville, Upper Canada, for not quite a year and a half. He had been the first minister called by that congregation after they had broken their connection with the Church of Scotland in 1844 and thrown in their lot with the Free Church. The fervour of that same disruption had brought James Nisbet from his home in Glasgow, Scotland, into the ministry of the Free Church in Canada. Missionary activity was not new to him. His brother was a Free Church missionary in the South Seas, and he himself had been active in church work and city missions. At 15 years of age, he had been a Sabbath School Superintendent. He was a carpenter and contractor, and he had intended to make his living at that trade when he came to Canada in 1845 at the age of 22. However, on arriving he had decided to devote himself to the ministry.[6] Now after twelve faithful years at Oakville, Nisbet had come to end John Black's eleven years as the solitary watchman in the West, and to enter with him on new ventures in mission.

Nisbet's coming, his zeal, his appeal to young people, his sharing of the services, all lifted the spirits of the minister and the people. Services could now be held weekly at the four 'stations' —Kildonan, Little Britain, Headingley, and Fort Garry. Nisbet's skills as a builder were put to good use also. The 1849 log school at Kildonan was in need of replacement; Black and Nisbet raised $1,000, and Nisbet designed a new stone school in which he did most of the carpentry works and made all the desks. (The building is still to be seen at Kildonan, and is known as Nisbet Hall.) At Little Britain Nisbet made some improvements to the meeting house, including a new front porch. He also drew up the plans for a stone church there. James Nisbet became one with the Kildonan folk in a different way when, like John Black, he married a young woman of the congregation, Mary McBeath.[7]

The two ministers continued their pressure for a mission to the Indians, and finally in 1865 the Synod agreed, and appointed James Nisbet as the missionary. One of Black's great plans had come to fruition, and the people had their outlet for mission. Enthusiastically they gave themselves to select a party to go with the Nisbets, and contributed generously to equip it.

At that time there was something of a gold rush along the Saskatchewan River and some of the Kildonan young men had gone to pan for gold. John Black had a pastor's concern for his boys, and this led to the decision that the mission to the Crees would be at the Saskatchewan River.

In retrospect, the sending out of their own mission was probably the high point in the life and work of the Kildonan congregation in the period when they were the leading edge of the Presbyterian Church in the North West. James Nisbet had been well briefed by John Black about missionary method but had made his own decision about the operation of the new enterprise. He would try a combination of direct personal evangelism among the roving bands, with a headquarters where there would be worship, instruction in farming, carpentry, and some regular school subjects. To implement all this would require a fairly large group, and they would have to be equipped with all that would be necessary for hunting, fishing, building, and farming, besides travelling equipment and household goods.

Preparations were under way in the fall of 1865, and in April 1866 John Black reported that the Kildonan people had contributed £80 to £100. It is easy to imagine the excitement and sense of involvement in the congregation as the outfit was systematically put together. John Black's letter to his brother continued:

> Letter from Saskatchewan last week. George Flett finally agrees to join Mr N. as interpreter, and an excellent one he is. You are aware that he is Mrs B's brother-in-law, and was with us in Canada in 1859. Mr N. has thus secured four of the best that this country offered: Geo. Flett, John Mackay, Alex Polson and Wm. McBeath. There will be no mission in the country better fitted with efficient men. John Mackay is a good Cree talker as well as fit for any kind of work. The other two, though not Crees, are good hands either at farm or carpenter work and are taken to help in building, breaking up land, etc. All are members of this congregation and of respectable families. George Flett already at work translating Psalms, etc. into the Cree tongue which is a beautiful language but encumbered with enormously long words i.e. VAWITCHE KECHE OOKIMA SKWAO (means) very great chief woman=Queen–rather exceptional.[8]

Indeed, the party was very much a Kildonan and family affair. Besides those mentioned in the letter there were to be Mrs Mary Nisbet and her baby; her sister, Christine, who was Mrs John Mackay, with their two children; and Mrs Mary Flett, who was the sister of Mrs John Black. The group left Kildonan on 6 June 1866 on horseback and in Red River carts. They had gone no farther than Headingley when they received the message that the younger sister of the two McBeath women and William had died, and their father would be alone. After much anguish and prayer they all agreed that their call was to go on with the mission, knowing that their father would be cared for by understanding friends. They began a journey of over 500 miles toward a people who had no idea they were coming, with no visible authority or protection, such as the Hudson's Bay Co. representatives had, needing to depend on the area for food, trusting in the good will of the Indians, and bringing them only a message of peace and a concern for their welfare.[9]

After the journey was over, Nisbet wrote to Sunday School pupils in the East, and included the following comment:

> We had a great many creeks and rivers to cross, and I dare say you would have been much amused had you seen the plans that were fallen upon for crossing such as were too deep for loaded carts. Few of my friends in the east have seen a boat made with two cartwheels tied together and an oilcloth spread over them, or one made of ox hides sewed together and stretched over a rough frame, that would take two carts and their loads at a tine. Such were the contrivances for getting over streams where there are no bridges or large boats by which we could cross.[10]

Forty days after leaving Red River the party arrived at Carlton House on the North Saskatchewan River where they camped for a week while Nisbet went searching for a suitable place for the mission headquarters.

GEORGE FLETT

George and Mary Flett met the group at Carlton House. George Flett, formerly the farmer of Headingley, had been recently in the service of the Hudson's Bay Company at Edmonton. It is illuminating to catch a glimpse of this man thirteen years before the beginning of his new career, as a measure of his spiritual journey during the years of John Black's ministry.

In January, 1854 Flett wrote to his brother-in-law, James Ross, in Toronto, about a visit he had recently made to Pembina, during which he had stayed with the Presbyterian missionaries at St. Joseph's. One of them asked Flett to come and work with them. He told Ross of an earlier experience at "Sault St. Mary" in 1835, concerning denominational rivalry. "All ministers of the Gospel," he wrote, "ought to come together and find out which is the true religion, and then come and tell us, then would we be willing to be Christians; but the way the ministers tell us, we do not know whom to believe...so we will keep our own religion. We Indians do not differ. We all hold to the same Great Spirit. Then said I, Friend, I cannot join you. To do good is not to speak evil of one another, and the Indians won't believe You,"[11]

It would seem that the witness of his wife, Mary, of her family, of John Black, James Nisbet, and of the Presbyterian community had led George Flett to believe them, and to become himself a witness to the Christian Good News among his own Indian extended family. He must also have satisfied himself that there would not likely be any competing mission. Neither George Flett nor his colleague of the half-blood, John Mackay, ever wavered from their commitment as preachers of the Gospel.

Nisbet returned to Carlton House with the word that he had decided upon a place sixty miles down the river, near the junction of the two great branches of the Saskatchewan. The Crees present objected to his announced plan of erecting buildings, ploughing fields, and taking possession of their land. George Flett saved the mission from this poor beginning. He was in the very area of his birth, and these were his mother's people. He claimed his portion of land, and then gave the Red River party permission to utilize his rights there. This claim seems to have been at once admitted by the Cree band.[12]

With the arrival of Nisbet and his closely knit group of Kildonan people at the place thus provided, there was at last a Presbyterian Mission among the Indians. They named their new headquarters "Prince Albert" in memory of the recently deceased Consort of Queen Victoria.

In his first pamphlet on the Indians, Lord Selkirk had said:

> …two different plans may be proposed. One is to employ missionaries to live among the wandering Indians, to gain their confidence, to take every opportunity of persuading them to adopt the practices, which are of most importance to their welfare. The other method is to establish a school…. A combination of these two methods would certainly be more effectual than either of them by itself.[13]

As over against Alexander Ross' plan in which missionaries would not be used until the Indians had learned to assure themselves of their daily bread, James Nisbet seems to have opted for Lord Selkirk's combination. Two small buildings were erected in the first year, and a larger one in the next year. A school was opened, and a farm was begun, and every means taken to attract the Indians to the place. There was some success, but the problem about which Mr Ross had warned arose quite quickly—the "praying keeps the pot boiling" attitude. Mr Nisbet was much concerned about how to deal with it. He also "lived among the wandering Indians" on the buffalo hunt. He held services both at Prince Albert and Fort Carlton, and he carried out an itinerant ministry which took him more than 400 miles up the North Saskatchewan to Fort Edmonton.

It seems obvious that such a multiplicity of tasks was far too much for even the most dedicated of witnesses to pursue for very long, yet that was the pattern of James Nisbet's life for eight years. For the first four of those years his only link with the Foreign Mission Committee of the Church was through John Black at Kildonan. With his old friend he shared the concern that as the Prince Albert area became attractive to more and more white settlers, the Crees moved farther and farther away taking their children with them; and this at the time when they were more in need than ever of mastering new ways of life, for it was becoming certain that their chief source of survival, the buffalo, would soon be gone. The long-planned entry of the Presbyterian Church into mission among the Indians came at a time of fundamental change for them; and this was a cause of deep concern to the two dedicated sponsors of the mission.

The Transfer, The Old Order Changeth

The departure of James Nisbet and his party of Kildonan missionaries did not mean that John Black was to be alone again. His protégé, Alexander Matheson, came home to Red River with his wife and two boys from Eastern Ontario. He had completed his College and University work in Toronto in 1860. He was called to Lunenburg in the Presbytery of Glengarry at that time, and was ordained there, thus becoming the first of the Red River people to enter the Presbyterian ministry. After serving at Lunenburg for six years, he came to his own. He was stationed at Little Britain, but his ministry extended to Kildonan (when John Black went to Fort Garry and Headingley) and also several preaching points in the Portage la Prairie area. The people there wished to call him as their minister, but at the same time he received a call from his former parish of Lunenburg. Because of his own ill health, and the unhappiness of Mrs Matheson and himself following the death of both their children to dysentery he decided, regretfully, to return to Glengarry in 1868. (Mr Matheson would come back to Red River from Lunenburg twice more during his ministry.)

Two men came to replace Alex Matheson; the Rev. William Fletcher came in 1868 from Carlisle in Western Ontario to the Portage la Prairie area; and in 1869, the Rev. John McNabb came to Little Britain from Luchnow, Ontario. Mr NcNabb was accompanied by Mr David B. Whimster, a theological student from St. Mary's, Ontario, who took charge of the Kildonan School. He would work with John Black at high school subjects in preparation for beginning a Presbyterian College. Mr Whimster also preached on Sundays, so was a very valuable member of the expanding ministerial team.

In an atmosphere charged with the expectation of union with the new Confederation of Canada, settlers and businessmen began to appear in the village of Winnipeg in the 1860s. The first newspaper, the *Nor'-Wester*, began in 1859. Though the settlers moved on farther, the village was growing. In 1868, John Black, with a grant of land from the Hudson's Bay Company and $400 from the Church in Canada, was able to open a small church building on

Thomas Douglas, Fifth Earl of Selkirk

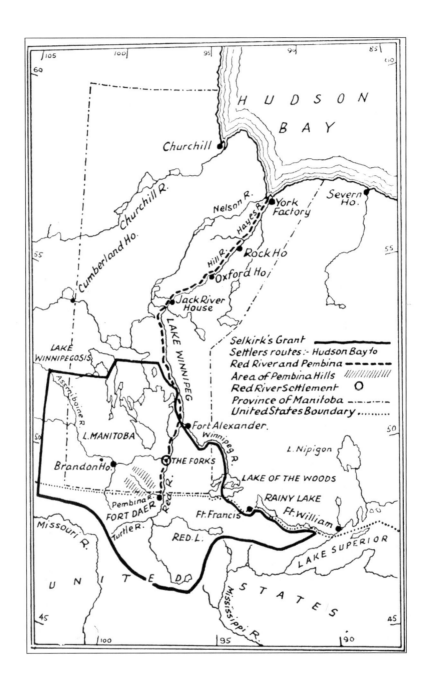

Map showing original tract of land granted to Lord Selkirk

Artist's sketch of Kildonan Church, 1860

Photograph of Kildonan Church, 1860

The Reverend John Black, 1880

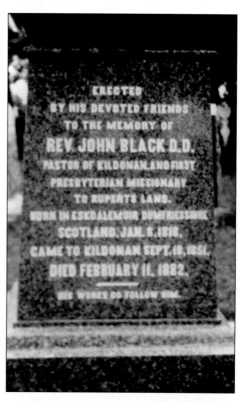

ERECTED
BY HIS DEVOTED FRIENDS
TO THE MEMORY OF
REV. JOHN BLACK D.D.
PASTOR OF KILDONAN, AND FIRST
PRESBYTERIAN MISSIONARY
TO RUPERTS LAND.
BORN IN ESKDALEMUIR DUMFRIESSHIRE
SCOTLAND. JAN. 8. 1818.
CAME TO KILDONAN SEPT. 18. 1851.
DIED FEBRUARY 11. 1882.

HIS WORKS DO FOLLOW HIM.

Kildonan Cemetery, just east of old church door

The Reverend John Black (1818-1882), first resident Presbyterian minister in the West

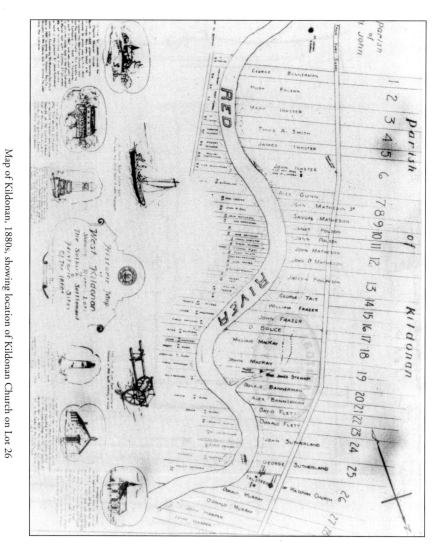

Map of Kildonan, 1880s, showing location of Kildonan Church on Lot 26

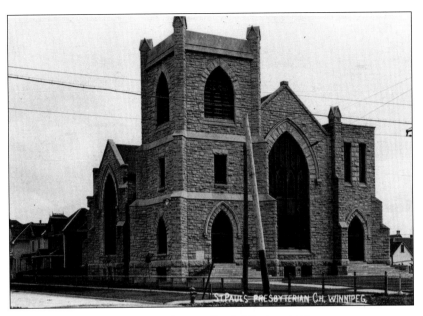

St. Paul's Presbyterian Church, Winnipeg, 1910

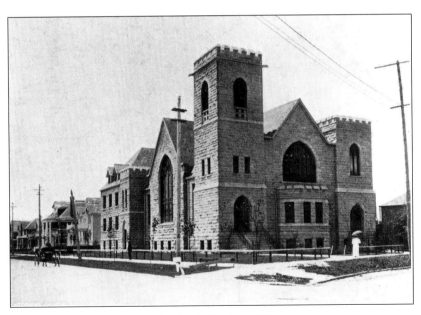

Elim chapel, Winnipeg, 1910

Old Kildonan Presbyterian Chuch, 1960s.
The walls of the church were stuccoed in 1921. The cemetery contains
the tombstones of many of the original settlers

Fort Street. The services there took the place of those which Black had held for years at the Court House at Fort Garry. He called the building Knox Church, after Knox Church in Toronto where he had been ordained, and where Dr Robert Burns had been the minister at the beginning of the Red River mission.

The late 1860s was a time of tension and anxiety for the people of the Red River area. They had come through a lengthy period of drought and grasshopper infestation in the earlier half of the decade. After some promising recovery in 1866-67, the year 1868 brought not only drought and grasshoppers again, but the strange failure of small game, the plains hunt, and the fish in the rivers and Lake Winnipeg. Relief came from St. Paul and other places in the United States in the form of food and seed wheat; the Hudson's Bay Company gave £6000, and help also came from Canada, A wave of sympathy for the starving, distant people was aroused both in Canada and in Britain.

In Upper Canada, farmers in areas that had become fully settled had long been interested in the promise of the prairies; and the Presbyterian, George Brown, in the pages of his paper, the *Globe*, in Toronto, had been extolling the virtues of the West for trade. Both of these initiatives had been consistently blocked by French Lower Canada's fear of such a massive extension of British Upper Canada's size and power. With the accomplishment of Confederation in 1867, however, the deadlock was broken; the West could join the Dominion as a separate entity—a land of opportunity for both farmers and traders. A few fortune hunters from Ontario appeared at Red River and became very strident in their promotion of annexation to Canada. Among these was the young doctor, John Christian Schultz. They became referred to as the Canadas, or the Canadian party. Farmers, with a natural loyalty to Canada settled along the Assiniboine in the Portage la Prairie area. (It was to some of these that Alexander Matheson, and then William Fletcher ministered.)

There was strong pressure for union with Canada from those who had signed the Petition of 1857. Many of these lived in the St. Andrew's-Little Britain district. The people of the St. John's and Kildonan area were basically in favour of union with Canada. In the village of Winnipeg there were some loud American voices speaking on behalf of hopeful businessmen in St. Paul and other places in Minnesota, urging annexation to the United States. The Canadian and British Governments entered into negotiations with the Hudson's Bay Company for arranging the transfer of Sovereignty and Government in the Hudson's Bay Territories to Canada.

The Canadian Government in 1869 began work on the long-desired overland route from Fort William to the West. As part of their Red River relief they decided on a job creation project: the Dawson road could be begun at both ends at once. The idea was sincere, and the road was needed—it would reduce the Red River–Lake Winnipeg–Winnipeg River route to Lake of the Woods by 110 miles. The intended effect of this good work was negated, however, by the insensitivity of the Canadian workmen who came in the spring of 1869 to stake out the claims. They began by buying out Indian land rights with a few bottles of whiskey. This gave rise to the fear among the Métis that the coming Canadian government would not, or possibly would not be able to, prevent an invasion of Indian and Métis rights. They decided then that it would be necessary, before a new regime became established, to ensure that the Indian title would be recognized and existing land claims safeguarded.[14] This basic attitude of distrust gave weight to remarks of contractors and their staffs about seizures of land and dispossession of old settlers as they were gossiped about. Dissatisfaction was expressed about rates of pay and method of payment, etc., and the underlying question was being asked; by what right did the Canadian government undertake this work when they did not own the country?[15]

There was indeed confusion and uncertainty about land rights; the *Nor'-Wester* newspaper and the Canadian party assured newcomers that the Hudson's Bay Company had no right to govern, and that land was as free for the taking as it had ever been. In 1863 the *Nor'-Wester* printed old Chief Peguis' claim that even the 1817 Treaty with Lord Selkirk had not constituted surrender of their lands, but that the annual gift of tobacco was intended only as a good will gesture until the Earl could return to negotiate. He never had returned.[16]

All of the old certainties were being attacked. No official word came to the Red River Settlement about "one of the greatest transfers of territory and sovereignty in history"[17] either from the Hudson's Bay Company, which for two hundred years had ruled the territory under licence from the Imperial Government, or from the Dominion of Canada, which, presumably, would soon become the government. No thought was given to negotiating, or even consulting with the people of the territory. "(The transfer) was conducted as a mere transaction in real estate."[18] While the white people and the English-speaking Halfbreeds seemed prepared to expect fair treatment under a new regime, the Métis were not. The real question, for them, was deeper than land rights. It was whether the people of the old settlement would control the new government, or the expected swarm of newcomers who could not be counted upon to guarantee their Church and language. Their fears were only increased when in August of 1869, without announcement, a party of Canadians began a survey which was perceived as threatening all land rights. Colonel Dennis, the leader of the survey, gave strong assurances, but, unfortunately, made them of no effect by his friendship with Dr Schultz, who made no secret of his contempt for the Métis nor of his expectation of being in the new government.

Under the leadership of Louis Riel, some of the Métis organized in the way they had long been accustomed to do for the buffalo hunt. They stopped the surveyors (who, following their orders, did not resist). Canada was not yet the government. When the *Nor'-Wester* announced that William McDougall had been appointed Lieutenant-Governor, to take effect when the transfer was announced, the Métis forced him to stay out of the territory, at Pembina, until the announcement was made. On 2 November 1869, they occupied Fort Garry. These steps were apparently taken in order to prevent the Canada party from cooperating with McDougall to frame a government before Métis and citizen rights could be negotiated.

The ensuing events are well known, and need not be recounted here; but the question is sometimes asked, where did the Presbyterians stand during the troubled ten months of October 1869 to July 1870?

On November 6 the village of Winnipeg and ten English parishes were invited to send delegates "to meet with the French on November 16 to consider the political state of the country and adopt measures for the future." On November 12 at Kildonan School, a public meeting was held of the inhabitants of St. John's and Kildonan Parishes, with John Fraser as Chairman and Bernard Ross as secretary. James Ross (who had returned to Red River, and had for some time been editor of the *Nor'-Wester*) was elected as the delegate for Kildonan.

Part of his instructions read as follows:

That in the opinion of the inhabitants of St. John's and Kildonan parishes it is a matter of regret that their French-speaking fellow settlers should have deemed it necessary to rise in arms and expel from the country the Hon. Wm. McDougall who was appointed by the Queen's Representative in Canada to the office of Lieut.-Governor of the country: and matter for regret also that they should have deemed it necessary to barricade the public highway, and seize on and search the property of members of this settlement while in transit along the said highway, seize and detain the mails, arrest and make prisoner one of themselves, and set a guard in, over, and around Fort Garry, the seat of Government.

That the inhabitants of the aforesaid parishes earnestly desire and hope that an arrangement may yet be come to, by which Lieut.-Governor McDougall might be admitted into the country and assume the functions of Government assigned him by our Sovereign's Representation in Canada.

That if after a fair and friendly conference all negotiations looking to the admission of the Governor fail, then it is the desire of the people of these parishes in order to prevent an interregnum or anarchy, that the present Governor and Council of Assiniboia be requested to continue to exercise their functions and to carry on the Government of this settlement until such time as some other constitutional or authorized Government take its place.

That a copy of these resolutions be furnished to our delegates for their guidance next Tuesday, and that said delegates in all other matters which may arise, act in accordance with the spirit and scope of said Resolutions.

Kildonan, Red River Settlement,
by order of the meeting.
James Ross, Esquire, Colony Gardens, Delegate for Kildonan Parish. [19]

In the negotiations which followed, it was Ross who became the principal debater with Riel, for both young men had gained their education in Canada; Riel in Montreal and Ross in Toronto. The English-speaking delegates could never quite rid themselves of a vague feeling that the erection of a Provisional Government was somehow illegal; but when it became apparent that the Hudson's Bay Company's authority, as represented by Governor William MacTavish, had really ceased to function, and no declaration had come concerning the Transfer to Canada, a Convention of forty (twenty French and twenty English-speaking) agreed to a Provisional Government. James Ross of Kildonan was Chief Justice in this Government and had a great deal to do with writing the Bill of Rights which the Convention approved. This document, somewhat added to, substantially became the Federal "Manitoba Act" of 1870, which created the "postage stamp" Province of Manitoba (about 100 miles square), while the rest of the Hudson's Bay Co. lands became the North West Territories.

On one occasion during the Provisional Government, Schultz escaped from jail in Fort Garry. He went to the house of Robert McBeth in Kildonan. McBeth did not especially agree with Schultz' politics, but did not refuse shelter to the fugitive. Schultz went on north to arouse the men of St. Andrew's, Little Britain, and the St. Peter's Indian settlement. Many of them, all armed, followed him to Kildonan school, where they joined another large company of men from Portage la Prairie and the Assiniboine settlements. These had been aroused by other escapees from jail—among them, Charles Vair and Thomas

Scott of the Dawson road party. These were all noisily determined to release all
the prisoners still held in Fort Garry, and to overthrow the Riel Government.
One Kildonan man, Hugh Sutherland, was accidentally killed in the excitement, and the Métis who shot him was beaten to death. When John Black and
other clergymen came with the news that all prisoners had been released, most
of the men dispersed.

It was probably a disgruntled Charles Mair whose report appeared in the
Toronto *Globe* of 28 March 1870, in which was said:

> The Protestant clergy are for 'peace, peace, when there is no peace' and
> to that cause and that cause alone, must be attributed the failure (of
> the movement)...if the Reverend Quartette had quietly studied their
> sermons, or in their closets offered a prayer for our success instead of
> going through the ranks discouraging our men, we would ere this have
> had the proud satisfaction of seeing 'the flag that braved a thousand
> years' floating over Fort Garry, and not be disgraced by that symbol
> of Jesuitical Fenianism that now hangs on the flag staff.[20]

It would be a mistake to think of the Riel period as mainly a French rebellion.
There was no disloyalty to the Crown. There was a feeling that the Hudson's
Bay Company had betrayed its people, and based on the insensitive behaviour
of the Canadian road builders and surveyors and the arrogance of the small
Canadian party, there was on the part of some a strong aversion to, and for
others a cautious hopefulness about becoming a part of Canada.

Judging by their names, many of the principals in the badly bungled
Transfer must have been Presbyterians: MacDonald, the Prime Minister,
MacTavish, the H.B.C. Governor, McDougall, the Lieutenant-Governor
designate, Donald Smith, the Head of the H.B.C. and Canadian Commis-
sioner, the Rosses, Frasers, Sutherlands, McBeths, and other "old settlers",
besides possibly Charles Mair, and Thomas Scott, the Ulster Protestant from
Ontario whose execution set his home province ablaze and pitted it against
Quebec in an early test of the new Confederation.

Those late sixties so fraught with change, were the last days of the isolated,
slow-paced Selkirk Settlement. A new act was about to begin, with many new
players upon the stage, and many of the others in the wings.

Among the first new players were the soldiers of the Wolseley Expedition
who came "with sword's loud clashing, and roll of stirring drum", but some of
whom were soon to be seen, under the guidance of John Black, putting the
finishing touches on the new Presbyterian Church in the little village of
Winnipeg, that all might be ready for the new day. Some viewers of the

changing scene voiced a fond thought, though, for the "good old days" of Kildonan:

> 0, for the times that some despise,
> At least I liked them, me whatever,
> Before the Transfer made us wise
> Or politics had made us clever.[21]

CHAPTER SIX

WITHIN THE BOUNDS: THE GENESIS OF A SYNOD, 1870-1884

THE YEAR 1870

1870 was a memorable year in the Christian world. In Rome, the Vatican Council decreed that the Pope was infallible. In Europe, it was the year of the Franco-Prussian war, which, though it was really of a nationalistic nature, yet carried Protestant-Catholic overtones. Presbyterians in Canada favoured the Protestant Prussians. In Canada, three political decisions opened the way for the new nation to stretch across North America filling the vast empty spaces. The settlements on the Red and Assiniboine rivers became the fifth Province of "Manitoba".[1] Rupert's Land became the North West Territories. With the promise of a railway, British Columbia decided that it would become the sixth Province.

In Toronto, the Canada Presbyterian Church, which for the first nine years of its organization had met only in its various Presbyteries and Synods, met for the first time in General Assembly. In terms of our story, the most significant act of that Assembly was to erect "a Presbytery in the Province of Manitoba" on 16 June 1870 specifying:

> That John Black, John McNab, William Fletcher, and James Nisbet, ministers, with their congregations, and Kirk Sessions be disjoined from the respective Presbyteries to which they belong, and that they shall form the said Presbytery, which shall be called the Presbytery of Manitoba...that the Rev. John Black shall be the first Moderator of said Presbytery, and that the first meeting thereof shall be held at Kildonan Church, Red River, on the first Tuesday of October next at eleven o'clock in the forenoon.[2]

Since Manitoba had become part of Canada, the responsibility for Mission work there was transferred from the Foreign Missions Committee to the Home Missions Committee. That same Committee had sent the first missionary to the Thunder Bay district in that summer of 1870. Mr Nisbet's mission among the Indians in Saskatchewan was left with the Foreign Missions Committee since it was an outreach to non-Christians. By 1870, Mission work was well established in British Columbia. This mission was left with the Foreign Missions Committee since that area was not yet part of Canada.

In 1870, the areas of Thunder Bay, Saskatchewan and British Columbia were scarcely aware of one another. Yet in each of these areas there was a developing Presbyterian Community. The year 1870 was significant for each. Though widely separated from each other, the narrow horizons of the Red River settlement were to be widened to include them. Soon they were all to be within the bounds of the huge Synod of Manitoba and the North West Territories.

BRITISH COLUMBIA

In 1862, James Nisbet came to Red River to assist John Black. He arrived by steamboat down the river from the rail terminus in southern Minnesota. That same summer the Overlanders, 150 Canadian men, women and children, arrived.[3] Surprised residents at Red River saw them only briefly. They were busy preparing to cross the prairies and the Rocky Mountains for Caribou Country. Gold had been discovered in the valleys of the Fraser and Thompson Rivers in 1857. By 1862, these valleys had become the Mecca of thousands of fortune hunters from California, the United States, and distant Canada. Few people chose the dangerous Overland route. Most flocked into Fort Victoria and Nanaimo on Vancouver Island or into New Westminster, the capital of the new Crown Colony of British Columbia. Many of these new arrivals pressed on to the gold fields. Others, hoping to profit from the prospectors, stayed on in the swelling towns. By the summer of 1857, Victoria had 30,000 people. There were Presbyterians on the Overlanders' steamboat, in the towns and up the rivers.

The Presbyterian churches were not by any means the first to appear on the coast. As early as 1836, the Hudson's Bay Company had an Anglican chaplain at old Fort Vancouver on the Columbia River. In 1837, two Roman Catholic priests arrived searching for French Canadians who had settled there after accompanying Alexander Mackenzie on his journey to the Pacific in 1793. Both churches were well established before the gold rush. Methodist missionaries came in 1859. All of these church representatives worked with newcomers and natives.

In 1861, the first Presbyterian minister appeared. He was John Hall, a minister of the Presbyterian Church in Ireland. He ministered in Victoria. In that year, the Canada Presbyterian Church was formed. They appointed Irish minister Robert Jamieson as a missionary to British Columbia. On the Roll of the Foreign Missionaries of the Presbyterian Church, Jamieson was listed as No. 20 and James Nisbet as No. 21. Jamieson reached the west coast in 1862. He was surprised to find John Hall at Victoria ahead of him. So he began his work at Nanaimo on the Island and at New Westminster on the mainland. From 1864 to 1867, he was joined by a Scot, Daniel Duff. During this period the two Crown Colonies were merged under the name of British Columbia. Victoria was its capital. New Westminster lost its special status. Duff was succeeded by another Scot, William Aitken, from 1868 to 1871. In 1870, the Canadian mission team consisted of Jamieson and Aitken. Robert Jamieson was to remain at his post for 22 years.

Meanwhile in Victoria, progress was being made. Two years after his arrival, John Hall saw the cornerstone of First Presbyterian Church laid by then Chief Justice, the Hon. D. Cameron. Two years later, in 1865, Hall sailed away to New Zealand. He was succeeded by a minister of the Church of Scotland, Thomas Sommerville. For unknown reasons, within a year, there was a split in the ranks of First Church. As a result, in 1866, St. Andrew's Church, Victoria came into existence with Sommerville as its minister. Three years later, in 1869, the Colonial Committee of the Church of Scotland sent Simon McGregor from East River, Nova Scotia. He joined in the work of St. Andrew's. During 1870, Sommerville departed for Scotland leaving the energetic and well-remembered Simon McGregor as minister of St. Andrew's.

When British Columbia agreed to become part of Canada in 1870 there was a flourishing evangelical ministry of the Presbyterian type both on the Island and on the Mainland. However neither the miners nor the natives had been reached.

THUNDER BAY

In recounting the story of the Riel government at Red River in 1869-1870, G.F.G. Stanley twice mentions the intervention of a Miss Victoria McVicar, a Canadian visitor to the settlement.[4] She successfully persuaded prisoners in Fort Garry to sign a promise to keep the peace in order to be released. She added her voice to those of several others pleading with Riel to save the life of Major Boulton. This vocal visitor was a Presbyterian and a member of a family which played a large part in the beginnings of the Presbyterian Church in Thunder Bay. Her father, Robert, who had died in 1864, was a Scot from the Isle of Islay.

He served the Hudson's Bay Company for many years. When Robert retired in 1859, the family settled at Thunder Bay at the mouth of the creek still called by their name. They were the first permanent settlers. They encouraged many Scottish families to settle there. Robert became the first postmaster. In 1870 his daughter Christina occupied that office. Victoria eventually succeeded her sister.

The walls of Old Fort William had been home to many Presbyterians ever since the great days of the North West Company and Lord Selkirk's visit half a century ago. In 1870, the Governor of the Fort was a Presbyterian, John McIntyre. As a young man, he accompanied Sir George Simpson on his round-the-world tour in 1840-41. After many years of Hudson's Bay postings, he settled with his wife and family at Fort William.

In 1868, a spectacular vein of silver was discovered on a little dot of an island across the bay. This place was called "Silver Islet." A mining community was quickly formed. Out of real concern for the spiritual and sacramental needs of such small communities of Presbyterians, John McIntyre, in 1869, invited his old friend Dr Alexander Topp, the minister of Knox Church, Toronto, to visit him at Fort William. Dr Topp conducted services and distributed sacraments among the Presbyterian communities.[5] When he left, Dr Topp promised to send a missionary to the Fort, the Landing, Silver Islet and to the road builders.

Dr Topp's request regarding Thunder Bay was responded to by the Knox College Missionary Society. They sent Edward Vincent, the first Presbyterian missionary to be appointed to the Thunder Bay area. Vincent had completed his summer ministry in 1870 when Dr Topp returned. Representing the Home Mission Committee, Dr Topp reported on his visit in the October 1870 issue of *The Home and Foreign Record of the Canada Presbyterian Church*. He wrote:

> For two or three months of the past summer, one of our students, Mr Vincent, was sent up by the Students' Missionary society. His labours were highly appreciated, and met with great acceptance.... Besides the want of divine ordinances the people in the localities labour under great disadvantage, that they have no provision for the education of their children.... They speak with much anxiety on the subject: and they would be glad, if any preacher coming amongst them might, in the meantime, do something to supply the want of a regular teacher.... It is about twelve miles across the bay; and for two months a preacher could cross in a sleigh on the ice, to conduct service with the miners.... The Protestant families at Fort William, and on the Kaministiqui River, and at Prince Arthur's Landing, are almost all Presbyterian. But

those belonging to other denominations concurred heartily in the desire to have religious ordinances at our hands, and promised their liberal support. And as the families (who are not numerous altogether) have agreed to raise $100 to $150 for the purpose of securing a supply of divine ordinances for the winter, I hope the Home Mission Committee will add what more is necessary, that a preacher may be sent to them before the close of navigation, in the end of October.[6]

The last months of 1870 brought another student, a Mr McFarlane, to Thunder Bay. At one time, he had been a tutor for the McIntyre family. He was able to fill the roles of both preacher and teacher in the winter of 1870-71.

As in the early days at Red River, it was the desire of the people that led to the founding of the Presbyterian Church at Thunder Bay.

ALONG THE SASKATCHEWAN

James Nisbet was at Prince Albert when he was named a minister of the new Presbytery of Manitoba. He communicated news of his Mission through long and chatty letters addressed to the children of the Sabbath Schools. These letters appeared regularly in *The Home and Foreign Record of the Canada Presbyterian Church.*

In the October 1870 edition, Nisbet's letter written the previous June, describes a colourful and ceremonial visit to the mission by a man of the Crees who regarded himself as a Christian leader. His followers had accompanied him. He used the Cree Syllabics to read the Scriptures. He had abandoned the common superstitions and professed to worship the one true God in the persons of the Father, the Son, and the Holy Spirit. He included many principles of morality. The centre-piece of the ceremonial visit was an elaborately carved peace pipe. The carvings represented, from top to bottom, the Father, the Son, the Holy Spirit, man, and "last of all, one to represent the devil as put under God and man, and all intended to set forth that peace should exist among all people."[7] This man had heard about the kindness of the missionary and his people to the Indians. He hoped that he and his followers might share in a little of it and "that they might get a taste of the things that grow out of the ground."[8] He informed them that he had taught his people all that he knew. He wanted to learn more so that he might be able to teach them more.

Mr Nisbet stated that he hoped that the figures on the peace pipe were not intended as objects of worship. Nisbet read the Ten Commandments to them. He showed them how much all people needed a Saviour. He urged them to accept the Lord Jesus Christ as their Saviour. The visitors were given food "that had grown out of the ground." Their leader received some Christian books in Cree. Mr Nisbet closed his letter:

> Now, dear children, you must help us to pray for this man and his followers. If he only knew and felt the truth more fully, he might be of great use on the plains, and his people might have influence with other bands of Indians; and you must help the Church to send another missionary or two here, so that I may be able to visit such people as these in their own camps on the plains, that they may have more frequent opportunities of hearing the word of life.[9]

Many children in the Sabbath schools of eastern Canada responded to such messages with interest and special offerings. These were regularly listed in the *Record* as "(Name) S. S. for Mr N." Thus the children had both a General Assembly Budget Allocation and an educational allocation.

Two other noteworthy events occurred through Nisbet's ministry in 1870. There was a terrible epidemic of smallpox on the plains in the summer. The Crees lost many people. The Reverend Nisbet was able to vaccinate some 200 to 300 people in the Prince Albert area and some at Carlton. In some manner, he came into possession of two smallpox scabs. Using a needle, he scratched the skin and rubbed the scratches with these scabs. By our standards today, it was a crude method but it gave results. This saved many lives in the area. Prince Albert was not affected as much as other parts of the west. In the same year:

> ...the missionary leader was able to prevent another possible tragic event. At this time the Hudson's Bay Company lands were transferred to the government. This led to unrest among the Indians. It was feared that they would eventually lose their lands and considerable grumbling and discontent was heard among the various tribes of Indians. It was feared by the authorities that there would be a repetition in Canada of the events that had recently taken place in the western United States, when the aroused Indians went on the warpath and wreaked vengeance on the settlers by wholesale slaughter. Nisbet was able to exert a steadying influence on the restless Indians by telling them that they would receive fair play by the...Dominion of Canada.[10]

The mission farm, which was intended to help make the project self-supporting as well as to teach the Indians to "grow things out of the ground," performed a vital role in the winter of 1868-1869 when there was widespread starvation on the plains. Over 1000 bushels of wheat, barley, potatoes, and turnips were given away to many who would otherwise have starved.

Nisbet's skill as a carpenter was put to the fullest use in the provision of residences, church, school, and grist mill. In every way that he could, Nisbet prepared for those who would succeed him. His main concern was to preach the Gospel and to show it.

A PRESBYTERY IN THE PROVINCE OF MANITOBA

Back at Red River, on 4 October 1870, the original western Presbytery met at Kildonan Church for the first time. Three ministers, Black, Fletcher and McNab met with three representative elders. The three elders chosen to represent their congregations in the new Presbytery were prominent men in the church and community.

The first elder was the Scottish patriarch of Little Britain, Donald Gunn. The 73-year-old Gunn had been in the North West for nearly sixty years. He had written a history of the Red River Settlement at about the same time as Alexander Ross (1856). In contrast to Ross, Gunn saw the Red River settlers as victims of Lord Selkirk's commercial ambitions. Gunn was the author of the 1857 proposal for amalgamation with Canada. Gunn was opposed to the despotic and unrepresentative government of the Hudson's Bay Company. He had been a member of the Provisional Assembly and hoped that a French-English balance might ensure peace. In the new province, he accepted an appointment to the Legislative Council.[11]

The other two elders in the new Presbytery were natives of the Red River, sons of Selkirk settlers. Both were farmers educated in the colony. Both men later moved to the east side of the river. John Sutherland operated a general store on his farm. He had become a member of the council of Assiniboia in 1866. He was a delegate from Kildonan in the Council of Forty. He was a leader in the Loyalist group and the Collector of Customs in the Provisional Government. Sutherland was appointed the first High Sheriff of Manitoba. Later he was appointed to the Senate in Ottawa. In 1870, the 49-year-old Sutherland worked for the founding of Manitoba College.

At 48, Angus Polson was well-known in the colony for his carpentry, especially furniture and spinning wheels. He was an able preacher, often occupying the pulpits of the growing number of congregations.[12]

Before these six men lay not only the care of the people at the eight preaching points within the new province and the distant mission on the Saskatchewan, but also the challenge of the new day. Kildonan Church was quiet and peaceful when they met that October day. However, a few months earlier it had witnessed the turmoil of the planned attack on Riel and the death of two young men in the midst of inflamed passions. It was only a few weeks since the hasty departure of Riel and the arrival of the troops. The British Regulars had departed but the Canadian volunteers were still at Fort Garry. There was as yet not peace between them and the Métis. The new Lieutenant-Governor, Adams Archibald arrived from Nova Scotia a month prior to the meeting of the Presbytery.

The Presbyterian community sent him a letter of warm welcome and were delighted to learn that he was a Presbyterian. He had begun the difficult task of organizing the new Province and North West Territories.

New settlers and speculators were arriving. Everyone expected many more to follow especially from Ontario. It was certain that among them would be numbers of Presbyterians. The new Presbytery had to be ready to make the Church accessible to these new settlers.

John Black, as Moderator, inaugurated the new Presbytery with a sermon on the text from Second Corinthians 4:1: "Therefore seeing we have this ministry, as we have received mercy, we faint not."[13] After assigning the ministers to their fields of labour, the first decision made was that meetings be arranged throughout the Presbytery to form missionary associations.

The second decision was to take a long step towards the cherished dream of a Presbyterian College. The Presbytery decided to ask the General Assembly for "a minister-capable of conducting the High School and preaching in the adjoining stations on Sabbaths." They proposed to pay one half of the stipend and to provide a house. They asked for a grant of the other half stipend from the Home Mission Committee in view of the proposed missionary labours. They requested that the Teacher, if possible, be here by the middle of July 1871. Meanwhile, the theological student, David Whimster, would continue to fill this position while continuing with his theological studies. The Presbytery assigned him courses and decided to examine him in three months, at the next meeting of Presbytery.

The three elders became a Property Committee. They were charged with seeing that the new Provincial Government provided proper title deeds for all Church properties. After assuring the existing congregations of the security of their home bases, the Presbytery would attempt to spread a growing awareness of the new Home Mission–Church extensions. They assumed that their request for a Teacher–Missionary would be granted by the General Assembly. They ended the year with a campaign to gather donations of both money and material for the building of a College at Kildonan.

Chapter Seven

The Period of the Presbytery of Manitoba, 1870-1884

The New Regime

The Presbytery of Manitoba was erected to coincide with the transfer of "Rupert's Land and the North West" to Canada. It was the organizational vehicle by which the Presbyterians carried out the work and witness of their Church during the decade and a half that saw the application of the Dominion Government's National Policy, the beginning and development of civil institutions in the Province of Manitoba and the North West Territories, the settlement of many people on the land, and the mushroom growth of villages into towns and even cities. This Presbytery served until its area was so huge and its congregations and missions so many that it had to be divided. It was separated into three Presbyteries bound together under a new Synod of Manitoba and the North West territories.

The National Policy

The National Policy was mostly the dream of a Presbyterian, Prime Minister Sir John A. Macdonald. British imperial trade preferences and American "Reciprocity" had ended. A union of all the British colonies in the northern part of the continent would form a strong British nation from coast to coast with a prosperous east-west trade. This would put an end to the dream of American annexationists on both sides of the border.

Prosperous east-west trade required a large population in the West. Therefore Manitoba and the Territories must be rapidly settled. The incentive was free land for homesteads. This required a survey of all the lands. In order to provide legal titles to the land, the Dominion Government, in the name of the Crown, would have to acquire title by agreement with the Indians. A railway was necessary to link east and west into one unit. It would transport both people and goods making possible the entrance of British Columbia into Confederation. A mobile police force would be necessary to guarantee law and order. It would represent the presence and power of the Crown throughout the wide area.

MANITOBA GOVERNMENT

The task of laying the foundations of representative government in the new Province were complicated by the rancorous atmosphere. In addition to the lawless confrontation going on between some of the Wolseley soldiers and Métis, the Roman Catholic Clergy and the 'Canadian' party were ready to put their respective pressures upon the new government. Riel was in the background, protected in Métis houses. Every settler, new or old, had only squatters rights to his land. Even Lord Selkirk's Treaty of 1817 was being challenged by the Canadian Party and by the Red River Indians. All Indians were confused and insecure before the mysteries of the impending rush of settlers. The situation cried out for impartial direction, for sensitivity with firmness and fairness.

THREE PRESBYTERIAN LIEUTENANT-GOVERNORS

The first Lieutenant-Governor of Manitoba was also 'ex officio' Lieutenant-Governor of the North West Territories. He was an excellent choice for the difficult task. The Hon. Adams George Archibald was one of the Fathers of Confederation. He was a native of Truro, Nova Scotia, a Presbyterian, a lawyer, and an experienced cabinet minister in that Colony. When the movement for union of the colonies began, Archibald was the Liberal opposition leader in Nova Scotia. He supported the Conservative Premier, Charles Tupper, regarding Confederation. Archibald took part in the conferences in Charlottetown, in Quebec, and in London, England which resulted in the British North America Act of 1867. Archibald was appointed Secretary of State in the first Canadian Cabinet. However, there was a strong movement in Nova Scotia opposed to Confederation. Archibald was defeated in the first election. He returned to the House of Commons in 1869 and to his place in Cabinet. His appointment as Lieutenant-Governor of Manitoba and the North West Territories followed in 1870. He arrived in Manitoba on 4 September 1870.[1]

In the beginning Archibald formed a Council with whose advice he ruled (so the phrase which is still in use, "The Lieutenant-Governor in Council", fully described his government). In his choice of Councillors, he kept a studious balance between French and English, Protestant and Catholic. This careful balance was not only the intention of the Manitoba Act, but was the only basis on which Confederation itself had been possible.

In order to establish a list of voters for a Legislative Assembly, a census was necessary. The result of the census is described as follows: Population of Manitoba, 11,963, of whom 558 were Indians, 5,717 Métis, 4,083 English Halfbreeds, and 1,565 white. Catholics numbered 6,247, and Protestants 5,716.[2]

On 30 December 1870, the first election sent twenty-four members to the Legislative Assembly, twelve English and twelve French. It was noticeable that in the election it was the vote of the 'silent majority' which carried the day. The extremists of both Riel's Provisional Government and the Canadian Party were not elected. When the Governor chose the members of the new Legislative Council (Upper House) he followed the same pattern.

By the end of the first Legislative Session, Manitoba had its basic statutes, an educational authority, and a judicial system. There were 26 school districts, of which sixteen were Protestant and ten Roman Catholic. The schools were the existing parish schools. Other such schools could be organized on local initiative. There was a Provincial Board of Education which had Protestant and Catholic sections. Provincial grants were distributed to the districts on an equal basis. The Rev. John Black was a member of the Board of Education.

The judicial system of the new Province was modelled on that of Britain. It was under the direction of the man who became the second Lieutenant-Governor of Manitoba and the North West Territories, Alexander Morris. Morris came from Ontario to be the Chief Justice of the Manitoba Court of Queen's Bench in 1872. He served in that office for only a few months because in 1873 Archibald resigned as Lieutenant Governor. Morris was appointed to replace Archibald.

No sooner had the volunteers of the Wolseley Expedition beed disbanded, when, in 1871, Archibald was faced with the threat of a Fenian Raid on Manitoba. They were a secret society of Irish-Americans who were using all means to overthrow British rule in Ireland. There had already been serious raids in eastern Canada. Manitoba was perceived to be a likely target. Archibald had only a newly formed twenty-man constabulary for defence. He called for volunteers and was gratified by the response. On one occasion he crossed the Red River to St. Boniface in order to inspect the Métis volunteers. He shook hands with the leader, who though carefully not named, was in fact Louis Riel. The Canadian Party made sure that this incident was well-publicized in Ontario. The storm that blew up in Ottawa eventually caused Archibald's resignation.[3] He later served as Lieutenant-Governor of Nova Scotia for ten years, was knighted, and served again in the House of Commons.

Archibald's successor, Alexander Morris, belonged to a family in Perth, Ontario which was active in the Presbyterian Church. His father, William Morris, had taken a prominent part in the struggle of the Church of Scotland Synod for recognition as one of the two Established Churches of Canada and, therefore, eligible for a share along with the Church of England, in the Clergy Reserves. He had been the Synod's Commissioner to take their petition to the Queen in London.[4] William's son, Alexander, after studies in Scotland, had become the first graduate in Arts of McGill College in Montreal. He later graduated in Law and served in the Legislative Assembly. He was Minister of Internal Revenue from 1869-1872.

In 1870 talk of the possible union of all the Presbyterian Churches was in the air. Alexander Morris, Dr Alexander Topp of Toronto, and Dr John Cook of Quebec were the small committee who arranged the time and place for a meeting of twenty-four delegates in September 1870. Their deliberations eventually led to the formation of the Presbyterian Church in Canada in 1875.[5]

Morris was Lieutenant-Governor from 1873 until 1877. Like Archibald, at least until 1874, he was the actual Head of Government. During the latter part of his term, government in Manitoba was headed by John Norquay, a Red River English-speaking Halfbreed.

At the end of 1873 the Dominion government of Sir John A. Macdonald fell. Alexander Mackenzie headed a new Liberal government. In 1875, the new government decided to take a step in the development of the North West Territories. Henceforth, they would have their own Lieutenant-Governor, but unlike Manitoba there would be no Legislative Assembly and no representation in Ottawa. Manitoba would develop as a Province but the Territories would continue to be directed from Ottawa with an administrative centre at Battleford.

Morris went to Toronto where he served in the Provincial legislature for several years. In 1880, he compiled a complete account of the western Treaty negotiations with the Indians with which he had been heavily involved. His book is still available today.

As an Indian Commissioner for the Treaties, Morris was responsible to the Dominion Minister of the Interior. In the Mackenzie regime this office was given to the Hon. David Laird who became the first Resident Lieutenant-Governor of the North West Territories.

David Laird was a native of Prince Edward Island. His father was a member of the Island's Legislative Council. David's education was at the Presbyterian Theological Seminary in Truro, Nova Scotia. He then became the publisher and editor of the Charlottetown *Patriot*. In 1864, Laird opposed Confederation. Prince Edward Island did not enter the Dominion. From 1871-73 Laird was the Liberal M.L.A. for Belfast, the area of Lord Selkirk's pioneer colony.

In 1873, he was an emissary to Ottawa to arrange for the Island's entrance into Confederation. When that was completed, he resigned his seat and was then elected to Parliament. His maiden speech in the House of Commons favoured the Opposition, over the Pacific Railway scandal. This scandal caused the fall of the Macdonald government. By the end of 1873, Laird found himself Minister of the Interior. Perhaps to familiarize himself with the Department, Laird, in 1874, had himself appointed as one of the Indian Commissioners for arranging Treaty No. 4 at Qu'Appelle Lakes.

It was following Laird's return to Ottawa, that the legislation was prepared which separated the government of the Territories from that of Manitoba. This was passed in 1875. In 1876, Laird resigned from the Cabinet and House of Commons. He was appointed Lieutenant Governor of the North West Territories and Indian Superintendent. While Government buildings were being prepared at Battleford, Laird and his staff were accommodated in the Swan River area, where the Hudson's Bay Company's Fort Pelly was located. A North-West Mounted Police detachment had recently been established there.

In 1877, the move to Battleford was accomplished. While the move was in progress, Laird became one of the Commissioners for Treaty No. 7, with the Blackfoot group of Indians in the south-west area of the Territory. By the time the treaty was signed at the Blackfoot crossing of the Bow River, Laird had settled at Battleford. Laird, the man from the smallest Province, had traversed on horseback hundreds of miles of Canada's largest domain.

Laird is described as a careful and methodical administrator. He was continually frustrated by the lack of Federal financial support and the inadequate arrangements for local involvement in government.[6] At the completion of his term in 1881, Laird returned to his newspaper in Charlottetown. However, 17 years later he moved to Winnipeg as Indian Commissioner for Manitoba and the Territories.

Laird was a good churchman. At Swan River in 1876, he found a Presbyterian minister, the Rev. Alexander Stewart, serving the Police, HBC Staff, Government Servants, and their families. When Laird was established at Battleford in 1877, he requested the Home Mission Board to send a missionary. The Rev. Peter Straith was appointed. Straith was ordained by the Presbytery of Manitoba in Winnipeg on his way to his station. In each of these ministries to the families of official people, the missionaries taught in the first schools for the transplanted children.[7]

The laying of the foundations of Manitoba and the North West Territories as parts of Canada was entrusted to these three capable statesmen and Presbyterians.

CHAPTER EIGHT

THE INDIANS, THE CROWN AND THE CHURCH, 1870-1884

THE TREATIES

The end of the centuries-old relationship with the Hudson's Bay Company as their trading partners puzzled and confused the Indians of the woods and plains. There was strong reaction at Red River to the very idea of the coming Canadian government. The Indians were alarmed. The expected throng of settlers reducing their living space, coupled with a growing realization that the buffalo would soon disappear, worried them. They recognized that there was a real possibility of homelessness in their own land and starvation.

In the far west, the Blackfeet and Crees were decimated by a fierce war between them in 1869-1870 over the dwindling buffalo herd and by the smallpox epidemic of 1870. The Chiefs and Headmen of the western plains were pleading for some protection from the American whisky traders whose vile brew was robbing and destroying their people.

The Indians living within the new Province of Manitoba were now claiming that Lord Selkirk's Treaty of 1817 was only a down payment and that Selkirk's early death prevented the completion of the Treaty. Pending a Treaty with the new government, they denied new settlers the use of land. They prevented settlers from cutting timber and interfered with the surveyors as they attempted to 'run their lines.'

Upon the arrival of Lieutenant-Governor Archibald in September 1870, the Indians pleaded with him to enter into a Treaty with them. They were promised negotiations in 1871.

Similar appeals from more distant bands reached the Governor in those formative years, pleading for arrangements that would assure their people of security of land and provisions.

Archibald reported to the Dominion government that, "The Indians of Canada have, owing to the manner in which they were dealt with for generations by the Hudson's Bay Company, an abiding confidence in the Government of the Queen."[1]

The authorities in Ottawa were aware that there were possibly 35,000 Indians in the former Hudson's Bay Company territories, as well as about 10,000 Métis, and not more than 2,000 whites. They were in dread of an Indian uprising comparable to the awful experience in the United States. It was desirable both at Red River and in Ottawa to begin negotiations quickly.

The Indian title to the land had been acknowledged since the British conquest of 1759. Indian Affairs were exclusively in the Federal jurisdiction by the British North America Act of 1867. The sole method of acquiring legal title to the land was to purchase the Indian title. In eastern Canada this had already been done by treaties which covered all the land as far west as the Lake Superior watershed. It was now necessary for the Crown to "extinguish" the entitlements of the Western Ojibwa (Saulteaux); the Swampy, Woods, and Plains Cree; some Assiniboins (Sioux relatives, also called Stoneys); some northern Chipewyans; and the Blackfoot Confederacy.

Beginning in 1871 at Lower Fort Garry, and continuing until the end of 1877, at a remarkable series of huge Indian gatherings, the Lieutenant-Governors and other Indian Commissioners conducted very tough negotiations with the elected leaders of all the Indian bands. Finally both sides invoked the same Great Spirit and hands clasped signed the Treaties Nos. 1-7. This forever changed the life of the Indians. They were assured of reserved land of their own choosing, cattle, seed-gain, implements, permission to continue to hunt and fish in the ceded territories until such time as they became private property, perpetual annuities for each person, special perquisites for Chiefs and Councillors, schools on the Reserves, and by request of several Chiefs, the prohibition of liquor on the Reserves.

It was difficult for the Indians to accept the strange concept of ownership of land, something which they recognized as the provision of the Great Spirit for their use. The payment by the government to the Hudson's Bay Company was a mystery to them. Their relationship to the Queen as Sovereign and loyal subjects, as Mother and children, was something to wonder about. Governor Morris explained that the gifts of the Great Spirit were for all people. Just as the Saulteaux had come from the east to live in the land of the Cree, so the whites had come. The Spirit had given one of the Queen's forefathers the right to govern the country. He had allowed he Hudson's Bay Company to rule in his name and to be the only lawful traders. The Queen had now taken the rule into her own hands. She had taken away the Company's trading monopoly. She had only compensated them for the loss of their benefits. Now she wanted many more people to share the lands. She wanted the Indians to put the rule into her hands as the Company had done. Their compensation was spelled out in the Treaties.[2]

By the time the seventh Treaty was signed, the North-West Mounted Police had been organized and dispatched to the Plains. They had effectively curbed the ruinous American liquor trade. They won the respect and trust of the Indians so that their example as agents of the Queen gave the Treaty Commissioners a favourable hearing.

The Commissioners were sincere in their concern for the Indians as they faced the approaching change in their way of life. They were certain that the settled life of the Reserves would benefit the residents. They were sure that the Indians would soon be self-supporting and become contented Christians and Canadians. Governor Morris, statesman and active churchman, at the completion of the Treaty process wrote:

> They are wards of Canada, let us do our duty by them, and repeat in the Northwest, the success which has attended our dealings with them in old Canada, for the last hundred years. But the Churches too have their duties to fulfil. There is a common ground between the Christian Churches and the Indians, as they all believe as we do, in a Great Spirit. The transition thence to the Christian's God is an easy one. Many of them appeal for missionaries, and utter the Macedonian cry, 'come over and help us'.

After listing some of the accomplishments of the Roman Catholic, Anglican, Methodist, and Presbyterian Churches, and naming some of their outstanding missionaries, including James Nisbet, Morris concludes:

> Let the Churches persevere and prosper.... Let us have Christianity and civilization to leaven the mass of heathenism and paganism among the Indian tribes; let us have a wise and paternal Government faithfully carrying out the provisions of our treaties, and doing its utmost to help and elevate the Indian population, who have been cast upon our care, and we will have peace, progress, and concord among them in the Northwest; and, instead of the Indian 'melting' away, as one of them in older Canada tersely put it, 'as sown before the sun', we will see our Indian population, loyal subjects of the Crown, happy, prosperous and self-sustaining, and Canada will be enabled to feel that in a truly patriotic spirit our country has done its duty by the red men of the Northwest, and thereby to herself. So may it be.[3]

With firm belief in the rightness of the British and Canadian cause, and convinced that the Indians were being sensitively provided for, the Indian Commissioners received clear title to the lands from the Lake Superior watershed across the 'fertile belt' to the Rocky Mountains, in the name of the Queen. Presbyterians had a great deal to do with the process.

Several names familiar to Presbyterians appear on the Treaties, as parties to them or as witnesses: Adams Archibald; Alexander Morris; David Laird; Donald Gunn; Alexander Muir, Sr.; George Flett; John McKay; Constable J.B. Mitchell, N.W.M.P.; Chief Keeseekowenin, Chief Okanes, Chief Wawaseecappo, and Chief Mistowasis.

Later the Indians learned by experience the severe restrictions exerted upon them by the Dominion Indian Act of 1876.[4] This Act was a gathering together of several existing Statutes in eastern Canada. By this most unusual Act, originally for their protection, some measure of control was placed upon practically every aspect of an Indian's life, including his or her very recognition as an Indian. The open discussion and decision, the high tone and spirit of the Treaty gatherings were negated for the Indians by this Statute. It governed their lives. This Indian Act was not too dissimilar from some British laws against the Scottish Highlanders after the defeat of Bonnie Prince Charlie. These laws were the direct cause of driving so many Scots to Canada and to their dominant roles in this story.

THE PRESBYTERIAN CHURCH

As the Indians went off to their reserved lands to learn the settled life, they were followed by missionaries of the various churches. Their object and desire was to win the people to Christ and to the Christian life. The churches were encouraged by the Government who saw the churches' efforts as the best way to civilize or settle the Indians and to keep the peace.

The first two Presbyterian missionaries of the new time were George Flett and his wife, Mary (Ross). Their term of service at the Prince Albert mission had come to an abrupt end after three years of strenuous work. Mary Flett was seriously ill and needed rest. They went off to their old home at Red River. They left behind them several evidences of their labours—new missions begun at Crowstand, Round Lake, Muscowpetung, and Piapet, all in the Saskatchewan country.[5]

Their leave of absence lasted five years. They were the worst years possible for finding rest and peace at Red River. The years 1869-74 were full of tension and turmoil. Mary's recovery was slow. George Flett joined his brother-in-law, James Ross, as a member of the Provisional Government under Louis Riel.

Together with the itinerant evangelist of White Horse Plains, James Tanner, they became the leaders and spokesmen for the English-speaking Halfbreeds. The three are credited with keeping the Anglo-Saxons and the French Métis from civil war and with restraining the Indians from joining the fight. As so often happens to peacemakers, they were distrusted by both sides. No place could be found in the new Manitoba Government for James Ross. He died shortly after at the age of 36. James Tanner became a candidate for Marquette in the first Legislative Assembly election. His wagon was surrounded by Wolseley soldiers whooping and firing guns wildly. The horses bolted. The wagon overturned. Tanner was dead. A fervent and respected voice for God among the Indians, whites and Halfbreeds was stilled.

By 1874 Mary Flett was sufficiently recovered to allow her and her husband to return to the missionary work. George was ordained a minister by the Presbytery of Manitoba. He was appointed to the Fort Pelly area north-west of the new province. They made their headquarters among Indian cousins of George. Their Reserves lay between Lake Audy in the Riding Mountain country and the Little Saskatchewan River near the present village of Elphinstone. George's mother, Margaret Whitford, an Indian girl of the plains, married George Flett, a Hudson's Bay Company Chief Trader. Margaret had a brother named Michael Cardinal, a great chief who took three wives—one Indian, one from Orkney, and one French. Their children, either full brothers and sisters or half-brothers and sisters to each other, were all full cousins to George Flett. Mekis, Okanase and Keeseekemenin were leaders of the Band, and signers of the Treaties.[6]

While the Fletts served at many places such as Rolling River and Wawaseecappe Reserves, their most effective work was at Keeseekewenin. They served the area for twenty-three years, 1874-1897. They had been at their post for ten years when the Synod of Manitoba and the North West Territories was formed in 1884. P.L. Neufeld, in the *Presbyterian Record*, quotes the Minnedosa *Tribune* in 1895 as saying:

> Faithful and persistent teaching and presentation of the gospel have effected wonderful change. Comfortable farm houses, well-tilled land, schools, churches, and progressive, intelligent, and contented people, respectable families, orderly church activities, clean tidy and well-clad children, and happy homes.[7]

Neufeld credits the success of the Fletts and other Presbyterian missionaries to two factors. First to their own racial background in both Indian and Caucasian cultures and their families' being leaders in both communities. The Fletts viewed prairie residents—Indians, Métis, or Caucasian—simply as 'People' among whom many would benefit from an encounter with Jesus Christ, and many of them did. Attendance at their services and other gatherings customarily included a cross-section of all these ethnic communities. When the first settlers from Scotland and Ontario arrived in the Elphinstone district, they found themselves invited to Communion in the Presbyterian Church led by Flett.

Second, to the team ministry of husband and wife, which was usual among Presbyterian missionaries, but was especially true of George and Mary Flett. Of enormous value in the Flett's ministry was their fluency in Cree and Saulteaux, French and English.

For James Nisbet at the Prince Albert Mission, the early 1870s was a time of stress. Besides the rigours of the many-sided daily tasks, in 1873 he received an official visit from a representative of the Foreign Mission Board, the Rev. William More of Ottawa. Nisbet learned, for the first time, that there had been persistent criticism of his priorities and of the small number of names being reported as converted after six years of work. Each member of the staff was queried. Mr Moore's report eventually gave much praise to Nisbet, but ended the Church's support of the farm. The Church was also made aware that much of the difficulty at the mission could have been avoided if they had sent a missionary from the beginning. Mr Moore, in fact, was accompanied by a second missionary with his young wife. After six years of pleading by Nisbet and John Black, the Church had heard the call. The new missionary was the former student minister at Thunder Bay, the Rev. Edward Vincent.

James Nisbet took the opportunity of Vincent's presence to journey with Mr Moore to southern Ontario. There, he saw some of his friends. He also conducted a highly popular tour of many Churches and Sunday Schools where he reported on the mission and thanked them for their support.

Métis people from Red River, very unhappy under the new regime, had been moving into the Prince Albert areas. Now, as a direct result of Nisbet's tour, settlers from Ontario began to arrive there. As they settled, the Indians withdrew to the west. They resented the newcomers' usurpation of their lands and the need to travel up to two hundred miles now to find the buffalo. The work of the mission became extremely difficult for Nisbet. It had changed from an Indian mission to a series of pioneer churches and preaching stations.

In the summer of 1874, Mrs Mary Nisbet's failing health was a matter of grave concern. She had shared all the hard tasks and difficulties of this mission with her husband. She was reaching the breaking point. Nisbet, his own health faltering, managed to take his wife and four children along the prairie trail to her father's home at Red River. Ten days later she passed away. James Nisbet's own condition rapidly worsened. On 20 September 1874, eleven days after his wife, he too passed away. John Black laid their bodies to rest in Kildonan churchyard. James Nisbet had been allowed for eight years to fulfil his life-long dream of preaching the gospel to unbelieving people. Nisbet had laid the foundation on which others could build.

Even as the Nisbets plodded their weary way to Red River from the North Saskatchewan, the Fletts began their new mission on the Little Saskatchewan.

At Prince Albert, Edward Vincent was succeeded by the Rev. Hugh McKellar in November 1874. McKellar later wrote of one of his unforgettable experiences:

> In the month of July 1875 we visited the Chief Mistawasis and his people while they were preparing pemmican and dried buffalo meat for winter supplies. The encampment was about two hundred miles south of Prince Albert. The day we left for our homes we witnessed a wonderful sight—an immense herd of buffalo grazing quietly in a valley of the south branch of the Saskatchewan River. Mr McKay told me it was a sight very few people (white and brought up in the country) had seen.[8]

Chief Mistawasis was a friend and admirer of James Nisbet and his brother-in-law John McKay from the earliest days of the mission. When the Treaty No. 6 was made with Lieutenant-Governor Morris at Fort Carlton in 1876, Mistawasis was the first of the Chiefs to sign it. When he had selected the site of his Reserve, about sixty miles up the river from Prince Albert, he requested the Presbyterian Church to appoint a resident missionary. He insisted that it be his friend, John McKay.

This "call" was recognized by the Presbytery of Manitoba. In 1878, John McKay, the veteran Halfbreed buffalo hunter from Red River, was ordained to his ministry at the Mistawasis Reserve. He and Mrs McKay (MacBeath) were still serving there when the Synod was formed in 1884.

The year 1878 was also notable for the arrival on the scene of the Indian work of two outstanding witnesses of the Gospel, Miss Lucy Baker and the Rev. Solomon Tunkansuyicye.

Lucy Baker, a woman from Glengarry, Ontario, acquired a rich education in Ontario, Montreal, the United States, and in France. While teaching school in Dundee, Quebec, she became a very active member of Zion Presbyterian Church. James Nisbet, at his distant post, was calling for someone with her abilities and interest to teach the Indian children at Prince Albert. The opportunity to respond did not present itself until after Nisbet's death. In 1878, her minister and his wife were appointed to Prince Albert. Miss Baker accompanied them. For some reason, at Winnipeg the missionaries could not or did not continue to their appointment. Miss Baker soon found a lady who was travelling to Edmonton whom she could accompany as far as Prince Albert. In October 1878, she made her home in the old mission house built by Nisbet. She began to teach the Indian children and others. At the founding of the Synod in 1884, Lucy Baker was still at her post. She was the first single woman appointed to the Indian missions.

In the same summer in which both James Nisbet and the Overlanders had arrived at Red River by steamboat (1862), the Sioux (Dakota) Indians were enraged at the quantities of wood being cut along the upper Red River to supply the never-ending appetite of the steamboats. They went on the war-path and massacred many white people, woodcutters, traders, missionaries, and others. Some of the Sioux fled across the border into the Assiniboine and Turtle Mountain areas. No amount of persuasion by either American or Hudson's Bay Company authorities could induce them to leave. Eventually they were given two Reserves, both on the Assiniboine River, one at Oak Lake and the other at Bird Tail Creek. Some of these Sioux people remained in the vicinity of Portage la Prairie. Others, later arrivals under Sitting Bull, elected to settle in the Prince Albert area. The Presbyterian Church has been in relationship to all of these Sioux immigrants since 1878. This phase of our Indian mission began when John Black and his Foreign Mission Committee of Presbytery were able to arrange for the appointment of a Sioux ordained Presbyterian minister, the Rev. Solomon Tunkansuyicye. He was transferred from the Presbytery of Dakota. He made his headquarters at the Bird Tail Reserve. He was a middle-aged man when he came. In his first letter to John Black, he announced his intention of visiting all the Sioux people in the new year. At the founding of the Synod in 1884, Mr Tunkansuyicye was faithfully at his special mission.

In the late seventies and early eighties other Indian missions were begun in the Saskatchewan country. The Rev. W.S. Moore was at Piapet, the Rev. Hugh McKay at Round Plain, the Rev. Ewen MacKenzie at Hurricane Hills, and the Rev. Mr Farrie at File Hill.

One of the earliest Indian Industrial Schools was established by the Federal Government a few miles west of Regina in 1880. It was placed under the care of the Presbyterian Church. The Rev. A.J. McLeod was the first Principal. Miss Bessie Walker was the matron.[9]

The Indian Mission was far from being the major activity of the Presbyterians during the fifteen years of the Presbytery of Manitoba. However, during those years of change in Indian life, there were Presbyterian people working along with the Indians. They built on the foundations laid by Selkirk, Ross,

Black and Nisbet.

When the Canadian Pacific train first went east from Winnipeg as far as Keewatin and Rat Portage (Kenora) in 1882, James Robertson was on it. He had recently been appointed Superintendent of Western Missions of the Presbyterian Church. When he met some of the Ojibwa people of the Lake of the Woods area, a seed was sown which would germinate into a whole new focus of gospel concern by the Presbyterian Church.

Chapter Nine

Manitoba College: Its Beginning and Development, 1870-1884

The idea of a Presbyterian College at Red River had been nurtured in the mind and heart of John Black ever since the day in 1854 when he learned that Presbyterians who had left St. John's Church to form Kildonan Church were no longer welcome to send their young people to St. John's College. For over ten years, he did what he could to teach them at his manse. It was not until the late 1860s that some of his people began to call for more formal secondary education. Black acted speedily. Still under the Foreign Missionary Committee of the Canada Presbyterian Church, he requested a high school teacher. It was in response to this request that David Whimster had been sent in 1869. He was using the old Kildonan log school during the Riel troubles. With Black assisting, Whimster taught Greek, Latin and Mathematics.

A provisional Board prepared and distributed a Prospectus for a College. The campaign for donations for a building at Kildonan was successful. By acceding to the new Presbytery's request for a Teacher-Missionary, the General Assembly of 1871 approved the founding of a College. The choice of the first Staff member was to be made by a Commission of two distinguished leaders of the Free Church—Dr Caven, the Principal of Knox College and Dr John Mark King, the minister of Gould Street Church in Toronto. Their choice fell on George Bryce, 27, a recent graduate of Knox College who had some experience as a high school principal. Bryce was born at Mount Pleasant in Upper Canada. He was a graduate of the University of Toronto in both Arts and Law. Many years later Dr Bryce, who remained at the scene of his pioneering labours for nearly sixty years, wrote:

> It was a rather dangerous experiment to choose a young beginner, but the venture was made, and Bryce, of Winnipeg, for the far west and George Leslie MacKay of Formosa, for the far east, were ordained together at the same meeting in Gould Street Church, Toronto. In

October (1871)...the new professor came west...and arrived in muddy Winnipeg which at that time had a population of 215 people in all. After eight o'clock on the evening of his arrival, he walked with his companion, the Rev. William Fletcher, from Fort Garry to the Kildonan manse, and took shelter with the Presbyterian pioneer, the Rev. John Black, in whose hospitable home there were eager discussions of the future for educational work and of plans for pastoral service.[1]

In that same month of October 1871, along with St. Boniface College and St. John's College, the Manitoba Legislature incorporated "The College of Manitoba".

The first home of the new College as such was in the large 'upper room' of the home of Donald Murray on the river lot next to and north of the Kildonan Church property. Professor Bryce taught a group of high school students whose numbers reached fifteen by spring.[2] David Whimster had gone for further study to Knox College in Toronto. During that first term of 1871-72, Mr Bryce became the first minister of Knox Church in Winnipeg, presiding over its organization.

After the end of that first term George Bryce left some of the men of Kildonan busily erecting the new two-storey log building that would house the College in the fall, and took the long journey back to southern Ontario. The General Assembly of the Canada Presbyterian Church was meeting in Hamilton. He was hoping that they would appoint an additional Teacher-Missionary for the College and Presbytery. In this he was disappointed. They were preoccupied with matters concerning the approaching union of the Presbyterian Churches and could not arrange for another Manitoba appointment. With union in the air, however, Bryce was urged to travel to Kingston where the Synod of the Church of Scotland was meeting. He made his request to them.

This time he was successful. The Synod appointed the Rev. Thomas Hart, M.A., as a missionary of the Church of Scotland to Manitoba. He would take part with Professor Bryce in the work of Manitoba College. The Synod of the Church of Scotland undertook to pay Hart's full stipend. This was a fine anticipation of the co-operative benefits it was hoped that the forthcoming union would bring.

Thomas Hart was a Scot who had been brought up in Perth, Ontario. He was a graduate of Queen's College, Kingston. After serving as Principal of the Perth Grammar School for several years, Hart went to Scotland for two years of post-graduate work. He was married at Perth when he returned from

Scotland. He and his bride journeyed to Winnipeg in time for the opening of the 1872-73 College term.[3]

The new building, clad in siding, stood on the Kildonan Church property near the river bank between the Nisbet stone school and John Black's manse. It offered enlarged teaching space and room for a residence. It had cost $4,200 to build. Over $2,600 had been gathered in gifts. $1,600 had been borrowed from the Hudson's Bay Company.[4] The Kildonan people and some recently arrived friends in Winnipeg had contributed a considerable amount in materials and labour. Bryce and Hart welcomed 24 students to the new College.

This pleasant and quiet academic scene at the old and hallowed Presbyterian centre was to be short-lived. By the end of the first term in the new College building, Professor Bryce was proposing to the Presbytery that the College be located in Winnipeg. During one year between the arrival of Bryce and that of Hart the population of the boisterous settlement lying north of Fort Garry and south of the old river front settlements had increased 1,000 percent. The population went from 215 to 2,000. There was a small boom in Winnipeg. Everyone's eyes were fixed on the future, a future in which Winnipeg would be a large metropolitan centre and the Gateway to the West. Business leaders, some of the old free traders and some recent beginners in trade, were pressing for the incorporation of Winnipeg as a city. Some of the necessities of city life began to appear. The Winnipeg General Hospital was opened. Banks appeared. Lumber and bricks were manufactured. There was much buying and selling of land. Houses and stores were constructed.[5] The first Methodist church was founded in 1871. In 1872, a small school was opened beside the church. By 1873, the school was too small.[6]

Kildonan Church and schools were about four miles from the scene of all this activity. St. John's Anglican College lay between. If Manitoba College was to effectively serve the Province and the Church, it must move to Winnipeg. This position of the two Staff members of the College was met by strong opposition from John Black and the Kildonan elders. The motion was passed by the casting vote of the Moderator. It was sent to the General Assembly of 1873 in Ottawa. Both Bryce and Black were there to present their opposing views. A commission of two ministers was appointed to assess the situation and report back. They recommended to the 1874 General Assembly that the College be moved to Winnipeg as soon as possible. They stated that:

WINNIPEG and not KILDONAN, is the place where the College should be situated. Whatever may have been the comparative claims of these places at the time the institution was first thought of, your commissioners can have no doubt as to which of the two preferences should be given under the changed circumstances of the country. The town of Winnipeg must soon be, if it has not already become, in strength and influence, the chief centre of Presbyterianism in the Province. The spirit and enterprise of the people of Kildonan in seeking to promote the interests of the higher education, and, in connection with these, the best interests of the Church, are deserving of all praise, and it is not without regret that a change is proposed which, if carried out, will inflict upon them serious disappointment.[7]

The Assembly agreed with the report. After only two terms at Kildonan, the College building was empty. The disappointment was indeed serious at Kildonan. People rallied and continued to send their students to their College. Later, John Black purchased the empty College building as a home for himself and his family after retirement.

In unintentional confirmation of the commioners' report that the chief centre of Presbyterianism in the Province was no longer Kildonan but Winnipeg, the Rev. Hugh McKellar, on his way in 1874 with the Rev. Hector Currie from Knox College to their first summer appointment in the West, wrote "Mr Currie preached in the Mother Knox Church, Winnipeg, on the 5th of July and it was my privilege to conduct the service in the same church on the 12th of July."

By the end of the final term at Kildonan three students were reported as ready for Theology. The Assembly was asked to permit them to take their course in Manitoba. Cautious approval was given. The same Assembly, in view of the approaching union, officially appointed Thomas Hart as Professor in the College. They also appointed a Board of 15 people to represent Manitoba. A.G.B. Bannatyne was Chairman. He served in this position for 14 years, long beyond the erection of the Synod in 1884.

Immediately after these important actions of the 1874 Assembly, the College moved to Winnipeg. After one term in a rented house, a larger building across the street was purchased for $4,000. This building, at the corner of Main Street and Henry Avenue, was the home of the College for six terms. When the C.P.R. tracks came marching across Point Douglas in 1881, they passed too near the College. The building was sold for about two and a half times its purchase price. A term was spent in a school near the present Manitoba Museum. Then, in time for the opening of the 1881-82 term, the College moved into a building prepared for it.

The Rev. J.H. Cameron, a young ordinand from Nova Scotia, was on his way to Oak River with his bride in the spring of 1882. It was his first western appointment. Cameron wrote of his honeymoon journey:

Winnipeg was reached in July, just after the big boom, and the big flood. The streets were a sea of mud, glazed shining black; but mud nevertheless and only needing a shower to make it glue. Not a block of pavement. Manitoba College was a lonely pile, away out on the prairie three or four blocks outside of the town....[8]

The site that could be so described in 1882 was chosen with wise foresight. It was the home of the College for over half a century. This site was on Ellice Avenue where the Federal Research Building stands. The main entrance of the College faced Vaughan Street. Its cost was ten times that of the earlier building.

At the opening of the 1874-75 term, in spite of his keen disappointment at the removal of the College from Kildonan, John Black volunteered to help in the teaching of Theology. This had been allowed by the General Assembly. Black was joined by the Rev. James Robertson, the new minister of Knox Church, Winnipeg. The two parish ministers continued this practice for six College terms. They helped to repay the College for the busy mission work being done by the Professors.

A significant development in the life of the College occurred in 1877. This was the formation of the University of Manitoba. The Lieutenant-Governor, Alexander Morris had considerable experience on the Boards of both McGill and Queen's Colleges. He wished to provide Manitoba with a University. At that time, the Province had arranged only for elementary education. All secondary education was conducted by the Church Colleges—St. Boniface Roman Catholic, St. John's Anglican, and Manitoba Presbyterian. It was necessary to arrive at agreed standards. The three colleges were far from any such agreement. They did not have all subjects in common. Those that were in common were often given differing emphases and importance. These differences were patiently and quietly resolved. In 1877, the University was chartered as a non-teaching body whose Council would be representative of all the chartered colleges, the university itself, and the Provincial Board of Education. Each College retained all its rights and privileges. The University had freedom to examine all candidates for degrees and to confer degrees. This did not apply to theological degrees.

The Governor General of Canada, Lord Dufferin, visited Manitoba in the year of the University's creation and in a speech at Winnipeg said:

In no part of Canada have I found a better feeling prevailing between all classes and sections of the community. This widespread sentiment of brotherhood is finding its crowning and most triumphant expression in the establishment of a University, under conditions which have been found impossible of application in any other province of Canada—I may say in any other country of the world—for nowhere else, either in Europe or on this continent, as far as I am aware, have the bishops and heads of various religious communities into which the Christian world is unhappily divided, combined to erect an Alma Mater to which all the denominational colleges of the Province are to be affiliated and whose statutes and degrees are to be regulated and dispensed under the joint auspices of a governing body in which all the churches of the land will be represented.[9]

The people connected with Manitoba College unanimously welcomed the development of the University. The College took a leading role in it from the beginning. The first University examinations were taken by seven students. All were from Manitoba College. The first B.A. degree of the University was conferred in 1880 on a student from Manitoba College, William R. Gunn.

The steady growth of the College was accomplished not only by a small staff and volunteers but by a Board of busy people who constantly wrestled with inadequate finances. Apart from the Professors' salaries, the first help from the church-at-large came immediately after the Presbyterian union of 1875. The General Assembly of 1875 established a fund of $3,500. As the needs of the expanding West came to be recognized, so did the importance of the College. The General Assembly of 1878 approved a fund of $100,000, "for Manitoba College, for requisite buildings, apparatus, library, and endowments." This fund still had to be raised, but the promise of it enabled the Board to make important decisions which resulted in the splendid building on Ellice Avenue. The cornerstone was laid in 1881 by the Governor General, the Marquis of Lorne. The College term of 1882-83 was held in it.

The end of that milestone term saw five young men completing theological studies under supervision of the Presbytery. The Senate of the College and the Presbytery approached the General Assembly of 1883 asking for a Department of Theology at the College. The response to this request was of great importance to the College and to the whole Church in the West. The Assembly asked their Moderator, the Rev. Dr John Mark King, to become Principal of Manitoba College and Professor of Theology.[10]

Dr King had been the minister of St. James Square Presbyterian church in downtown Toronto for twenty years. The congregation had outgrown Gould Street Church where they were meeting when Dr King had recommended George Bryce as the first Professor of Manitoba College. Before going to Gould Street Church, Dr King had been minister of Columbus and Brooklyn, north-east of Toronto. He was born in Roxburghshire, Scotland in 1829. He came to Canada in 1856 after receiving his M.A. from Edinburgh University and graduating from the United Free Church College. It was after two years of post-graduate study in Halle, Germany that he began his ministry in Canada. In 1882, he published his *The Characteristics of Scottish Religious Life and Their Causes*. He received the Doctor of Divinity from Knox College Toronto.[11] The General Assembly had honoured him with their highest gift. They called him to go to the distant West to teach many of those who would be the teachers and leaders of the Church.

Dr Bryce recalled many years later that:

> With Scottish caution (King) did not at once accept the offer of a College position but came out to Manitoba to look over the ground. He went as far west as Indian Head (the limit of the railway at the time) and after full investigation decided to throw in his lot with the new country. And having once made up his mind, he never looked back. From that day he gave all his powers to the land of his adoption and the College of which he was the head.[12]

Dr King's first term at the College, 1883-84, ended as the Presbytery requested General Assembly to divide its territory between three new Presbyteries and to erect a Synod over all. The request was implemented in 1884. During the decade and a half of the Presbytery of Manitoba, the Church College had developed from being only a fond hope in the mind of John Black to a small but strong arm of the Church with a distinguished and devoted staff. It was housed in a building designed for future growth. It graduated both ministers for the expanding Church and scholars holding respected University degrees for the West, or wherever they might choose to serve.

While celebrating his thirtieth year of ministry at Kildonan in 1881, John Black, the pioneer and planner, was able to see the rising walls of the new Manitoba College. However, the call to leave his earthly labours came early in 1882 before the new College opened.

CHAPTER TEN

FINDING PRESBYTERIANS: THE HOME MISSION, 1871-1884

DIVIDE AND CONQUER: THE WESTERN SURVEY

On the Trans-Canada Highway West, at Headingley, near the western edge of the City of Winnipeg, the traveller sees a sign reading 'Principal Meridian 2 km'. Following this direction, one is led to a cairn bearing a message in bronze. A basic fact of the utmost significance to every inhabitant of the country through which the traveller will pass is given expression here—the fact of the Land Survey.

The Dominion Government, contrary to the practice in the earlier Provinces, retained in its own control all the Public Lands of Manitoba and the North West Territories. As noted earlier, the survey of Canada's new jurisdiction began even before the Transfer, in 1869, and played its part in causing the Riel resistance, and was stopped. The survey was delayed for two years. It was resumed in July 1871, just as the Indians in the Province of Manitoba were being summoned to treat with the Lieutenant-Governor and the Indian Commissioners for the surrender of their lands.

The "great lone land" was to be conquered by dividing it into quarter section plots one-half mile square and containing 160 acres each (comparable to the system in the United States). The "Sections" were one mile square, and contained 640 acres. They would be grouped into a square measuring thirty-six sections and entitled a "Township". The townships would be numbered from south to north, beginning at an east-west base line. These columns or "Ranges" of townships would be numbered east or west from a north-south base line. The obvious east-west line was the 49th parallel of latitude—the United States border. The north-south, or longitudinal, base line was fixed by the Surveyor-General, Lt. Col. J.S. Dennis, at ten miles west of the Red River at the U.S. border (so as to avoid the band of trees along the river). When approved by the Dominion Government, this line, projected north, became the Principal Meridian; and every rural address in Western Canada was determined by its position on this grid. Gerald Friesen, in his history of the Canadian Prairies, describes this benefit of the square survey:

> A farm at SE6, 2–4, W1 (the southeast quarter of section 6, township 2, range 4, west of the first meridian) was twenty-three miles west of the prime meridian and six miles north of the forty-ninth parallel. An iron stake driven into the ground by the surveyers to mark each unit as they staked off the surface of the plains became the reference point for every pioneer, the solution to almost every dispute about boundaries.[1]

The survey proceeded speedily to cover all of the original Manitoba, and then continued westward until it reached even into British Columbia.

LAND USE

Even as the Indian Treaties were being negotiated, and the survey was under way, the Dominion Government was widely seeking settlers for the west by offering free homesteads on the millions of acres available. The Canada Homestead Act of 1872 made it possible for persons over eighteen years to take up 160-acre homesteads. After three years of residence, titles would be issued. In addition, each family could obtain a preemption on another 160 acres for $1.00 per acre. The offer was genuine, but not by any means all of the newly surveyed acres were available for free homesteads. There were substantial subtractions to be made first.

The lands which the Indians would choose for their Reserves would be part of the surveyed grid. Not all of the lands were part of the square survey; the "old settlers" were confirmed in the possession of their long, narrow farms along the rivers, and the length of these was eventually agreed to be four miles. The new survey had to be fitted around them. The Manitoba Act of 1870 gave 1,400,000 unspecified acres to the unmarried children of Métis families. The survey made it possible for these to be located; but this provision was very controversial, and by the time all of the grievances were settled, not only the parents of the Métis children were included in the land offer, but also all the old settlers of every kind. The total was to reach 2,448,160 acres. Another commitment made before the survey was to the Hudson's Bay Company. Part of the Transfer compensation was to be in the form of land grants; some of these would be surrounding the Company posts, but one-twentieth of the fertile belt would also be reserved for the Company, subtracted in small parcels from the available land.

There were new costs for the development of the west, which were also to be paid through grants of land; two sections of every Township would be reserved for school purposes; and part of the expense of the vitally necessary Railway would be paid with 25,000,000 acres of "land fair for settlement"; these, and assorted other costs were to be paid by land grants. The result was that only the even-numbered sections were made available for settlement. This meant that many of the expected settlers would not be able to find available free land, but might buy their homesteads from any of the reserved lands that would be for sale.

THE NEW SETTLERS, 1871-1875

Manitoba was now a part of Canada, and the new Presbyters found themselves dealing with a branch of the national church with which they were not familiar, the Home Mission Committee. (The Pacific Coast Mission remained under the Foreign Mission Committee since British Columbia was not yet a part of Canada; and so did the Indian Mission, as it was to unbelievers.)

As Manitoba became organized, and the National Policy began to take effect, more and more people made the arduous journey to claim the promised land.

They came mainly from Eastern Canada, many from Lanark County in the Ottawa Valley, and from the Georgian Bay area. Some also came from Britain and Europe. Single men, young couples and whole families travelled by train to the end of steel in Minnesota. Then the steamboats would puff their path down the winding Red River. Some would leave the boat as soon as it crossed the border at Emerson. They would assemble their outfits and travel along the Border Commission trail. Some would find their journey's end in the Pembina Valley, others would press on over the escarpment to the Turtle Mountains and beyond. Most of the passengers continued on to The Forks of the rivers at Fort Garry. They would then complete their outfits in the bustling new Supply Centre of Winnipeg. Some chose to go east of the river where the Survey was completed early. They were soon joined by some of the old settlers. John Gunn from Little Britain located there and so did John Sutherland, the Presbyter. Their property at Lot No. 2 of Lord Selkirk's plan was expropriated to make room for the coming Canadian Pacific Railway. The district, called Springfield, became the first Rural Municipality in Manitoba in 1873. The park-like land was very attractive to Ontario farmers whose former farms had required much clearing. Some newcomers went south by the old buffalo hunters' trail to the Boyne River area. Some chose the North-West, the Stony

Mountain District, long the source of building stone.

Many who settled near Winnipeg were Presbyterians and longed for the Church in their new communities. The Presbytery ministers, professors, students and elders did their best to provide services. Rev. Alexander Matheson, John Black's protégé, spent most of his ministry in his home area and did much to develop the new congregations. More and more of the newcomers took the Portage Trail along the Assiniboine and the Whitemud Rivers. The borders of the "Postage Stamp" Province were soon crossed and settlement began in the North West Territories. Winnipeg, the focus of all this arrival and departure, grew rapidly and incorporated as a City in 1874. An event notable in Presbyterian development was the formation in 1875 of The Presbyterian Church in Canada by the union of the various Synods in the Eastern Provinces.

Forty-four years later Dr George Bryce, who served in the West for over 50 years, began a series of History Reports appended to the Synod Minutes, and wrote from his own experience. Extensive use of these reports has been made in this section.

In the 1920 report the following list appeared to show the growth of the Presbytery of Manitoba between 1871 and 1875.

LIST OF MISSIONS, 1876-1881

In the year 1871, almost at the beginning of the half-decade we are considering, the list of Missions was:

Kildonan	John Black
Prince Albert, Sask.	James Nisbet
Portage la Prairie, etc.	William Fletcher
Little Britain, etc.	John McNabb
Manitoba College and Winnipeg	George Bryce

In 1875 the list had grown to the following proportions:

Kildonan	John Black
Emerson, Roseau and Pembina	John Scott
New Westminster, B.C.	Robert Jamieson
Little Britain, Selkirk and Park's Creek	A. Matheson
High Bluff and Portage Creek	Alexander Frazer
Knox, Winnipeg	James Robertson
Poplar Point, Ossowo and Baie St.Paul	S. Donaldson

Rockwood, Dundas, Greenwood and Grassmere	A.Glendinning
Prince Albert, Sask.	Hugh McKellar
Portage la Prairie and Burnside	Allan Bell
Okanase (Indian)	George Flett
Fort Pelly, Sask.	Alex. Stewart
The Boyne and Pembina Mountain	J.S. Stewart
Manitoba College	George Bryce
Manitoba College	Thomas Hart

Vacancies: Palestine, Woodside, Golden Stream and Westbourne, Springfield and Sunnyside, Headingley and Riviere Sale, Clear Springs and Caledonia.

In the 1875 list, Professor Hart, formerly of the Church of Scotland, had become a member of the Presbytery of Manitoba. Also, since British Columbia had joined Canada, the Rev. Robert Jamieson at New Westminster is included in the list. Dr Bryce commented that this listing was purely formal, since as far as practicable routes were concerned, British Columbia was farther away from Winnipeg than was Quebec or Scotland.

Of the ministers named on this list six had been received in 1875. Bell, Glendenning and Scott were in regular pastoral work. Jamieson was in B.C., Flett was in Indian work, still under the Foreign Mission Committee. Stewart was the Chaplain at Fort Pelly, the temporary capital of the North-West Territories. The vacancies listed are in Springfield, Stony Mountain, along the Assiniboine and the Whitemud. They are the places that the professors, students, and Winnipeg ministers tried to serve regularly.

Only two of the churches at this time were self-supporting—Kildonan and Knox Church, Winnipeg. With George Bryce as their minister the latter congregation grew. Their church building was enlarged twice, until it held over 400 people. In 1874, the Rev. James Robertson, from Norwich, Ontario, accepted a temporary appointment to serve the new fields, but Knox Church gave him a hearty call. He gave his boundless energy to all aspects of the work, as did Dr Black at Kildonan.

The transfer of the West to Canada, and the building of the Dawson Route caused a major shift in the migration pattern of the overflow populations from eastern Canada and from Britain and Europe. For years the United States had been the goal. Thousands of experienced farmers and their families had settled in Michigan, Wisconsin, Minnesota and Kansas. Now they came to western Canada. In addition to all those who used the rail and steamboat system, there were many who came by covered wagon, driving their cattle, and bringing their furniture. The Hudson's Bay Company, being primarily interested in the fur trade, had always discouraged the use of the land for farming, except for the riverside communities. Now some enterprising newcomers tried farming on the plains. Soon they were dotted with new shacks set widely apart on the checkerboard of the Survey grid. Many felt that however good it might be where they were, it must be better farther on. The Qu'Appelle Valley was reached, then the Saskatchewan as far as Battleford, and even Edmonton. Only the mountains stopped the westward trek.

THE CHURCH RESPONDS

Many newcomers were used to fully developed churches and they longed for the comforts of religion. The small group of ministers and others in the river settlements were kept working as hard as possible to try to meet this desire. They were under some pressure because, while the Home Mission Committee was generous with financial aid, the local leaders were expected to urge the new congregations to become self-sustaining as soon as possible. They did their best, but sometimes there really was no prospect of permanence. In the Pembina area, for example, there were two flourishing centres, Mountain City and Nelsonville. When the Canadian Pacific Branch line reached the area, it went between these communities; whereupon the houses and businesses were moved to the railway and became the town of Morden.

No less than nineteen churches were built in this period: nine in 1879 and ten in 1880. Mr John McKay, a wealthy Montreal merchant, was very generous in his support of this project. Mr J. Mather built the first church in Keewatin, and Mr Robert Campbell, a retired Hudson's Bay Company Chief Factor, built a church at Totogan from his own resources. Totogan was the site of a bridge crossing the Whitemud River between Westbourne and Lake Manitoba. Mr Campbell came to Red River in the 1830s when the Hudson's Bay Company tried to establish a sheep ranch. He went with a small group to Kentucky to bring back a flock of sheep. They lost most of the sheep on the long walk back. The experiment was abandoned and Campbell was transferred to the fur trade division.

Working out from Fort Simpson on the Mackenzie River, he and a small party actually ascended the Liard River which tumbles into the Mackenzie from the mountains. He found two other rivers at the top—the Stikine, flowing to the Pacific Ocean, and the Yukon (which he called the Pelley). He established a Hudson's Bay Fort on the Yukon which he named Fort Selkirk. During a terrible winter there, in near starvation, and in danger from hostile Indians, his Diary recorded his regular devotions. He looked to John Black at Kildonan as his minister, and is buried in the churchyard there. At Totogan, Campbell was in competition with another Presbyterian, Peter McArthur. McArthur established a landing for his lake boats which brought fish, timber, and gypsum from as far north as Winnipegosis. He was very generous in the building of the Presbyterian Church there. McArthur had been one of the original survey party working on the Dawson Road. They so alarmed the Métis that the Riel resistance followed, and McArthur spent some time in jail in Fort Garry. Both Totogan and McArthur's Landing are long since gone.

At the end of this period, Dr James Robertson organized the Church and Manse Building Fund, and through his canvassing raised $53,000 in 1881. Presbyterian churches in Scotland and Ireland were concerned about the emigrants going to Canada and were regular in their support of the new work in the West. Dr Sprott, the minister of North Berwick in Scotland, visited and later gave enthusiastic lectures in Ontario and Scotland about the opportunities of the West.

This five-year period ended with the Presbytery recording 29 ministers in pastoral work, in addition to the two Professors. They were finding Presbyterians and had gathered them into 43 organized congregations which had a total of 156 preaching points. They were ably assisted by students from Manitoba College and from the East. Dr Bryce recalled what happened during one College Christmas break:

> From the 28th of December to the 13th of January, two professors and one theological student drove 470 miles, preached 14 sermons, gave in addition, 9 religious addresses, baptized 8 children, visited numerous families, organized a mission, and opened a church.

At the far edges of the West there was similar activity. The Church of Scotland continued its support of the work in British Columbia. There were six ordained ministers at Victoria, Nanaimo, Comox, Langley and Nicola. Robert Jamieson, the solitary minister of the Canadian Church at New Westminster, joined his Scottish colleagues in their Presbytery.

At Lake Superior, after several short-term student appointments, the Rev. Donald McKercher served from 1873 until 1880. Besides his regular pastoral work at Port Arthur, Fort William and Silver Islet, he had services among the men building the Dawson Road. He then followed the same pattern along the Canadian Pacific Railway until it reached half way to Winnipeg. Beyond that, the Rev. A.H. Cameron had groups of workers at 27 points all the way to Rat Portage (Kenora). In Knox United Church, Kenora (which used to be Presbyterian) there is a beautiful round window depicting the Burning Bush.

For years it was hidden by decorative organ pipes, but a renovation revealed it. Also revealed was the story of how it came to be there. It was a gift of appreciation by Chinese workers for the Railway Camps Ministry.

From Silver Islet to Battleford the distance is over 1000 miles. It could take nine weeks for Winnipeg to receive an answer to a letter. It was obvious that the far-flung field required constant attention. At the urging of the Presbytery (which was given Synod powers in 1875) the General Assembly agreed to the new position of Superintendent of Western Missions in 1881. The obvious choice was the Rev. James Robertson, who had been the very active minister of Knox Church, Winnipeg, for seven years.

CHAPTER ELEVEN

THE NEW SUPERINTENDENT AND HIS MEN, 1881-1885

Presbyterians always look for a Higher Hand that guides in the affairs of men, and especially in His Church. The combination of James Robertson and the task of Superintending the Western Missions is an unquestioned evidence of God's Providence.

Born in 1839, James was the third son in a small-farming family. The village in Perthshire, Scotland was called Dull, but James was anything but that. When the family moved to south western Ontario in 1855 to begin a new life, James carried a high recommendation from his teacher. After sharing fully in felling trees and preparing the land for cultivation, he began to attend school. This meant walking six miles to Woodstock and back each day. When an examination for a Teaching Certificate was announced, the minister of the Presbyterian Church helped him to use his recommendation to become eligible for the test.

He won his Certificate. He was about 17 years old, and began to teach in a rural school nearby. In the home where he boarded, he met his future wife, Mary Anne Cowing.

James became aware of a group of Gaelic-speaking Highland folk in Woodstock who had no minister. He "had the Gaelic" so he became the regular preacher to them on Sunday afternoons. This was in addition to his Sunday School class. This experience, no doubt, helped him years later when he found other Gaelic Presbyterians in Western Manitoba. James taught school later at Innerkip, but Mary Anne sensed that his real desire was to become a minister. When she promised to wait and pray for him, there began a ten-year period of preparation. James graduated from the University of Toronto and from Union Theological Seminary in New York. He worked there in an inner-city mission.

James and Mary Anne were married and his first parish was a three-point charge at Norwich, Ontario. After about three years there, in 1873, Mary Anne again realized his restlessness. They had three little boys by this time, but Mary

Anne supported him in taking a six-month appointment to Manitoba. He was to serve developing new communities. He visited and preached along the Assiniboine and Whitemud Rivers as far as Palestine (Gladstone) for about six weeks. The distance was 100 miles west of Winnipeg. Then came his call to be Minister of Knox Church, Winnipeg.

The growing congregation had recently called the Rev. William Cochrane, a prominent minister in Brantford, Ont. He had been a visitor on behalf of the Home Mission Committee. He had declined the call. Then there was a division in the congregation; some wished to call a minister from the Church of Scotland. Others wanted to remain with the Canada Presbyterian Church (the Free Church). It was 1874, only a year before the Union which would create The Presbyterian Church in Canada. They called James Robertson, who was only 100 miles away. James evidently had fallen in love with the West. He accepted the call. Seven busy years later, he was invited to make the whole of the West his own, and to claim it for the Lord and for his Church.

There was considerable opposition at first to the creation of such an un-Presbyterian office, so it was hemmed-in by a number of restrictive rules. These the new Superintendent usually kept; but sometimes he would act on his own "to get something done that had to be done". Of course, there was criticism, not only about the office, but also about how James Robertson managed it. He entered his new position with his usual zest, and gradually he won the trust of the Church.

As far as the Ministers and the Missionaries in his expanding field were concerned, he always had their love and loyalty; he was not only a shepherd to the scattered flock, but to the under-shepherds as well.

The stories of this remarkable body of men are full of adventure, privation, appointments kept with difficulty and much expenditure of energy. The men are far from complaining, though; they were a team of western witnesses to the Lord.

In his first report, Robertson emphasized his preference for young single men for pioneer work. They would have more strength and stamina than older men; and be more mobile than married men with families. Robertson, himself, was a young man of 42 years when he became Superintendent. He was often far from home. He was a faithful letter-writer, often sharing the adventures of his days' travels.

One of the team was Hugh McKellar, another Scottish emigrant. He was two years younger than Robertson. When he graduated from Knox College, Toronto, in 1874, he was one of two graduates sent out by the Student Missionary society. He was appointed to Prince Albert to replace James Nisbet. When in Winnipeg on his way, he preached at Knox Church just before

Robertson was inducted. His companion, Hector Currie, also preached at Knox. He was going to replace Robertson at Gladstone. McKellar, at Prince Albert, told of seeing the huge buffalo herd with John MacKay and Chief Mistawasis. When Robertson became Superintendent in 1881, McKellar was at High Bluff, Manitoba, where he remained for twelve years. He married while there in 1881. After pastorates in Ontario, he became part of the Foothills Missions, in south western Alberta. In 1924 McKellar published a most informative book. He had corresponded with as many of "Robertson's Men" as he could contact, asking them to send a picture and an account of their service in the West, and to let him know of anything remembered. The response was large and appreciative. The book is packed with pictures and stories that tell of the western witness. The book is called *Presbyterian Pioneer Missionaries in Manitoba, Saskatchewan, Alberta and British Columbia.* The list at the back of the book contains 165 names. Many of these served before and after the five-year period we are now considering. Typically Dr McKellar did not include his own story, but on the back pages of the copy that was loaned to me, a friend has written a sketch of his career.

Not all of the pioneers were young men. Dr Bryce has mentioned several men in middle life whose ministry makes one wonder at their stamina and energy.

Hugh Jamieson Borthwick was 52 years old when he came to the Boyne and Pembina region of Southern Manitoba in 1876. His previous ministry had been among the lumber-jacks in the backwoods of the Ottawa Valley. He had entered the ministry in middle-age after a distinguished career in education. He had been principal in three grammar schools in Ontario, in Newmarket, Kingston and Ottawa. He had been Inspector of Schools in Ottawa. Both he and his wife, Marion, had come from the Edinburgh area of Scotland. They had five children. The following note about Mr Borthwick appears in the 25th Anniversary report of Knox Church, Morden, Manitoba in 1911, by Dr M.C. Rumball, Pastor:

> When he (Mr Borthwick) began work in Manitoba, if he had not Wesley's parish, he had as much of it as one man could well be expected to look after. It extended from the Boyne River to the southern national boundary, and from near the Red River to the Turtle Mountains, about 3,200 square miles. Many are the interesting tales the veteran can tell of the early days. He would gather a few children together, teach them through the week, preach on the Sabbath, and then off to another settlement to do the same. Thus he covered the ground, fording streams, wading sloughs, facing storms,

he carried the Gospel message to the lonely settlers.

In 1885 Mr Borthwick was the first Moderator of Rock Lake Presbytery. After 1911 Mr Borthwick became the first School Inspector in Southern Manitoba; for three years he was editor of the Morden *Herald.* He died at Morden in 1916 at 92 years of age.

CHAPTER TWELVE

THE NEW SYNOD

A Scottish nobleman, Lord Elphinstone, visited Manitoba in 1879. Driving along the old Carlton Trail on his way to Riding Mountain he passed new settlers building their isolated houses. One man, working on his roof, called out "Is this Sunday?" The visitor's comment was that when there are no schools or churches, you don't even know what day it is.

In the years 1881-85 there was indeed a great need for churches, and even a great demand for them. Immigration was still increasing. The Canadian Pacific Railway had reached beyond Calgary. Branch lines were being laid in Manitoba. People were settling along the railways. New communities, even towns, were appearing. Winnipeg had its speculative land boom. Newcomers still pressed on beyond the railways, so new areas of isolation were created. James Robertson tried to reach people in all of these situations. He helped them gather into congregations. He needed leaders for them. He visited Colleges in the East and in Scotland and wherever he might find recruits for his band of missionaries in the West. He invited, he urged, he begged, he appointed men to the ever-expanding settlement.

On the field his constantly repeated motto was "Visibility and Permanence". The result was that Robertson and his men were seeing 30 to 40 churches and manses being built each year of this period. Almost all of them were made possible by the Church and Manse Building Fund.

As far as Church organization was concerned, these busy years revealed that the Presbytery of Manitoba was no longer adequate; it had become too unwieldy. As the settled area widened, and as Dr Robertson was successful in his quest, more and more ministers were added to the Presbytery, and, of course, an equal number of Elders. It became clear that several smaller Presbyteries would serve the large area better. For a time General Assembly resisted this idea, but in 1884 the Assembly agreed. In 1881 there had been 32 ministers on the Roll; in 1884 there were 66. There were to be three

Presbyteries—Winnipeg, Rock Lake, and Brandon. Together they would comprise the Synod of Manitoba and the North West Territories. The Presbytery of Winnipeg included the Lake Superior area. The Presbytery of Rock Lake covered all of southern Manitoba. The Presbytery of Brandon consisted of all the rest of the West, even including British Columbia.

The new Synod met for the first time as such at Knox Church, Winnipeg, in 1885. The Canadian Pacific Railway Company offered free transportation. There was a spirit of optimism and hope.

The first Moderator of the Synod was Professor George Bryce, D.D. He had been the first new member added to the original Presbytery in 1871. He had taught long hours in the College, and had seen it grow. He had prepared Knox Church for its first full-time minister. He had made those long expeditions for preaching, visiting, baptizing. On one occasion he had followed the Dawson Route by road, lake and river, all the way from Winnipeg through North West angle and Fort Frances to Port Arthur. "Finding Presbyterians" was gratifying because of the welcome he received. Dr Bryce well deserved to be the first Moderator of the Synod. The first Clerk was another veteran, the Rev. D.B. Whimster. Mr Whimster was the theological student who first taught the classes at Kildonan, which developed into Manitoba College. He had completed his studies and was serving as a minister.

As the Moderator constituted the new Synod with prayer, the Ministers and Elders would be aware that they were Christ's servants who had been put in charge of the Western Witnesses from Silver Islet to Vancouver Island; from Emerson to Edmonton, and from Manitoba College to Mistiwasis Reserve, all now within the bounds of the Synod of Manitoba; and that the one thing required of the man in charge is that he be faithful to his Master. (From I Corinthians 4:1 and 2.)

EPILOGUE

On a September afternoon in 1940, I approached Kildonan Church for the first time, to attend a meeting of the Presbytery of Winnipeg. As I passed the historic gravestones, the church door opened, and out stepped a tall military officer wearing a clerical collar. "I'm Sam Farley," he said, "Minister of First Presbyterian Church in Regina, and now a Military Chaplain. Who are you?" I gave him my name, and told him I was a student for the ministry from Toronto, appointed to Gonor across the Red River from Lower Fort Garry and Little Britain. "Follow me," said Mr Farley. I followed him past the stones of the pioneers, Bryce, Ross and Black, until we stood before the large stone bearing the name "Robertson". "Read, mark, learn, and inwardly digest," ordered the Chaplain, "if you intend to be a Presbyterian Minister in the West!" I obeyed.

This is the inscription:

The Reverend James Robertson, D.D.
1839-1902
Pastor of Norwich, 1869-1874
First Pastor of Knox Church, Winnipeg
1874-1881
Superintendent of Missions
1881-1902
Endowed by God with extraordinary talents, entrusted by
His Church with unique powers, he used all for the good of his
country and for the Glory of God. The story of his work is the
history of the Presbyterian Church in Western Canada, and while
Western Canada endures that work will abide.

To his memory and to the Glory of God this stone is erected
by a few of those who loved him and counted it a joy
to labour with him in his great work.

Mr Farley then showed me the inscription on the other side of the stone. It is in memory of Mrs Robertson who kept home and hearth together for him and their family while he was far away. Beside the big stone is a little one—Willie.

Quietly then we went into the old church to be about our Father's business.

Around me, both inside and outside, was the evidence that this was the first Presbyterian church west of the Great Lakes. I already had some evidence of that earlier time.

Beside the All Peoples Mission which I was serving lived Mrs Mary McKenzie, its founder. She had served for many years with her husband, the Rev. Ewen McKenzie at the Hurricane Hills Indian Reserve in Saskatchewan, an extension of James Nisbet's pioneer Mission.

In "retirement" she was a witness to the children of Red River people, who belonged, but rarely attended Little Britain Church and Sunday School. They had responded, and had brought their Ukrainian and Polish playmates. There was also a Sunday School held in a summer cottage which belonged to the Rev. George Gunn, a retired Presbyterian Minister who belonged to Donald Gunn's family.

I had spent the previous year 1938-39 as Student Missionary at Knox Church, Morden, and Mountain City. There I had learned about the pioneer work of Rev. Hugh Borthwick. Following that memorable moment at Kildonan, I became a student at the United College, the amalgamated version of Manitoba College.

My first appointment as an ordained minister was at George and Mary Flett's field at the Okanais Reserve, and the village church in Elphinstone. On the wall of the old church on the Reserve was a large framed picture of Professor Thomas Hart of Manitoba College. Now one could remember how it came to be there. Later I was minister of St. John's Presbyterian Church, Winnipeg. The church building stands at the border which divided the old parishes of St. John's and Kildonan. In 1969, St. John's and Kildonan became a two-point charge. Thus for 11 years I had the privilege of being the minister of Kildonan Church.

The unique work of James Robertson was providential for its time, a time of many witnesses for a rapidly expanding Church. This is an attempt to fill in the background, and to tell of some of the earlier witnesses. It only deals with the early part of Dr Robertson's work. The rest of the story, and all that has followed, begs to be told.

The visitor to Kildonan today will find a bridge crossing the river where the ferry used to go. The bridge is called Settlers' Bridge, and the road is named for Chief Peguis, who was such a help to the Selkirk Settlers, whose family names are remembered there.

There is a new church building now, to serve a new community; but firmly attached to it is James Nisbet's 1864 stone school, serving as the Parish Hall.

ACKNOWLEDGEMENTS

I appreciate very much the faithful support of this project by the Synod of Manitoba and North Western Ontario and its History Committee, Jean Campbell, and James Garnett.

I also acknowledge with my thanks the help I have received from friends in St. John's Presbyterian Church, Winnipeg, Noreen Allan, Vic Sheddon, Elveretta Smith and Doris Binding; from Robert Kennedy, in Winnipeg; Gordon McCutcheon in Thunder Bay; and Norma Proudfoot in Edmonton. Last but not least my wife Irene and my son David.

END NOTES

Chapter 1: The First Presbyterians, 1700-1810

1. W. Stanford Reid, ed., *The Scottish Tradition in Canada* (Toronto, 1976), 31.
2. John S. Moir, 'Enduring Witness', *The Presbyterian Church in Canada* (Toronto, 1975), 51.
3. *Ibid.*, 65.
4. *Ibid.*, 17.

Chapter 2: Lord Selkirk and Assiniboia, 1771-1822

1. J.P. Pritchett, *The Red River Valley, 1811-1849* (New Haven, 1942), quoted from Lord Selkirk's papers, St. Mary's Isle, 17.
2. Following the collapse of the highland uprising, 1745-46, in an attempt to restore the Stewarts to the throne, the British Government moved to end the old Clan system with its first loyalty to the Chief, who could raise his own army at will. The Chiefs became owners of great estates. On these weresmall farms leased from "the Laird" by tenant farmers. The Lairds tended to become absentee landlords, and in time came to believe that the raising of sheep would be a more profitable use of their lands than small farming. The tenants were thus forced off the land and out of their homes. This action was known as the Highland Clearances.
3. George Bryce, *Life of Lord Selkirk* (Toronto, 1912), 13.
4. *Ibid.*, 14.
5. Chester B. Martin, *Lord Selkirk's Work in Canada* (Oxford, 1916), 17.
6. Pritchett, 22-23.
7. *Ibid.*, 25.
8. *Ibid.*, 25.
9. Bryce, 16.
10. Pritchett, 26.
11. *Ibid.*, 26.
12. *Ibid.*, 28.
13. Patrick C. White, 'Introduction' from *Lord Selkirk's Diary, 1803-04* (Toronto, 1958), xxiv.
14. Manitoba Legislative Libary (MLL), Selkirk, Thomas Douglas, 5th Earl of, 'Observations on the present state of the Highlands of Scotland, with a view of emigration' (Winnipeg, 1806).

15. Metropolitan Toronto Library Board (MTLB), Selkirk, 'Observations on a proposal for the civilization and improvement of the North American Indians within the British Boundary' (Toronto, 1807), 17.
16. Pritchett, 36.
17. W.L. Morton, *Manitoba: A History* (Toronto, 1967).
18. Manitoba Library Association (MLA), *Pioneers and Early Citizens of Manitoba* (Winnipeg), 89.
19. Alexander Ross, *The Red River Settlement* (London, 1856), 31.
20. *Ibid.*, 31.
21. *Ibid.*, 47.
22. A.L. Farris, *A Short History of the Presbyterian Church in Canada* (Toronto, 1975), 43.
23. Ross, 31.
24. Anne M. Henderson, *Kildonan on the Red* (Winnipeg, 1981), 55.
25. Provincial Archives of Manitoba (PAM), Selkirk Papers.
26. Alexander R. Sutherland, *The Selkirk Settlement in Red River*, frontispiece.
27. George Bryce, *John Black, Apostle of the Red River* (Toronto, 1898), 49.

Chapter 3: Alexander Ross and a Congregation-in-Waiting, 1822-51

1. "Their task was to settle in the Church (in England) such a government as may be most agreeable to God's holy word, and most apt to procure and preserve the peace of the Church at home, and nearer agreement with the Church of Scotland, and other Reformed Churches abroad." ('Ordinance calling the Westminster Assembly', quoted from W. Beveridge, *A Short History of the Westminster Assembly* [Edinburgh, 1904]).
The Assembly had the active involvement of Commissioners from the Church of Scotland, which was already reformed. The productions of this assembly are collectively called the Westminster Standards. They consist of: the Confession of Faith, the Directory for Public Worship, the Form of Church Government, and the Larger and Shorter Catechisms. Although these Standards were met by discord in England, they were welcomed in Scotland as hopefully leading toward the unity of the church in England. They became the recognized "Subordinate Standards" of the Church of Scotland. Of these Standards, by far the most widely-known is the Shorter Catechism, which soon reached nearly every home. It is a manual for instruction in the basic doctrines of Christianity in question and answer form.
2. "Man's chief end is to Glorify God, and to enjoy Him forever.... God's works of Providence are, His most holy, wise, and powerful preserving and governing all His creatures, and all their actions.... Sin is any want of conformity unto, or transgression of, the law of God.... The only Redeemer of God's elect is the Lord Jesus Christ, repentance unto life, with the diligent use of all the outward means whereby Christ communicateth to us the benefits of redemption...the Word ...the Sacraments...Prayer..." (quoted from W. Beveridge, *A Short History of the Westminster Assembly* [Edinburgh, 1904]).
3. Kenneth M. Haig, *What Mean These Stones?* (Winnipeg, 1951), 12.
4. *Ibid.*, 14.
5. *Ibid.*, 15.
6. *Ibid.*, 16.

7. G. Hutchinson, 'British Mehtodists and the Hudson's Bay Company, 1840-1854,' W.L. Butcher et al. eds., *Prairie Spirit: Perspectives on the Heritage of the United Church of Canada in the West* (Winnipeg, 1985), 29-30.
8. *Pioneers*, 219.
9. Haig, 19-20.
10. *Ibid.*, 28.
11. PAM, Ross Papers, C14.
12. Manitoba Department of Tourism and Cultural Affairs (MDTC), 'Nisbet Hall,' Historic Resources Branch (Winnipeg, undated).

Chapter 4: John Black and Kildonan Church, 1851-1870

1. University of Winnipeg Archives (UWA), John Black Letters #8 (Winnipeg, 1851).
2. P.L. Neufeld, 'John Tanner,' in *Presbyterian Record*, Sept. 1978.
3. J.W. Bond, 'Minnesota and its Resources,' from W.L. Morton's *Introduction to Eden Colvile's Letters, 1849-52*, Hudson's Bay Record Society (London, 1956), xxiii.
4. *Ibid.*, xxi.
5. Bryce, 70.
6. Bond, cx.
7. Bryce, 67.
8. Haig, 31.
9. M.E. McBeth, *The Story of Kildonan Church* (Winnipeg, 1984), 7.
10. Bond, cv.
11. PAM, Ross Papers, Wm. Ross to James Ross, Nov. 4, 1853.
12. *Ibid.*, Jan. 31, 1854.
13. McBeth, 8.
14. PAM, Ross Papers, John Black to James Ross, May 31, 1854.
15. McBeth.
16. Neufeld.
17. PAM, Ross Papers, William Ross to James Ross, Nov. 4, 1853.
18. Bond, liii.
19. Bryce, 81, 84.
20. UWA, Black Letters #27, Nov. 1, 1862.
21. *Ibid.*, #26, Apr. 3, 1861.
22. PAM, Ross Papers, Feb. 7, 1855.
23. UWA, #15, Sept. 21, 1854.
24. *Ibid.*, #18, Nov. 8, 1856.
25. *Ibid.*, #22, Aug. 8, 1857.

Chapter Five: A Presbyterian Mission Among the Indians

1. Bryce, 26.
2. MTLB, Selkirk, 'Observations on a proposal for the civilization and improvement of the North American Indians within the British Boundary' (Toronto), 1, 2.
3. *Ibid.*, 3-5.

4.   Ross, 1.
5.   *Ibid.,* 322-23.
6.   D.O. Jones, 'Knox Presbyterian Church, Oakville, Part II' from *Presbyterian History,* 26, 3 (Oct. 82), 3.
7.   Bryce, 93.
8.   UWA, John Black Letters #33, Apr. 16, 1866.
9.   Bryce, 95.
10. *Ibid.,* 97
11. PAM, Ross Papers, George Flett to James Ross, Jan. 26, 1854.
12. Bryce, 98-9.
13. MTLB, Selkirk, 8-9.
14. Morton, 118.
15. Bryce, 107.
16. A. E. Thompson, *Chief Peguis and His Descendants* (Winnipeg, 1973), 32.
17. Morton, 117.
18. *Ibid.*
19. PAM, Ross Papers #372.
20. Quoted from G.H.G. Stanley, *Louis Riel* (Toronto, 1963), 105-06.
21. Morton, 150.

Chapter Six: Within the Bounds: The Genesis of a Synod, 1870-1884

1.   G.H.G. Stanley, *Louis Riel* (Toronto, 1963), 124, 131.
2.   United Church Archives (UCA), *Presbytery Minutes, 1870-1875* (Winnipeg), 1-2.
3.   Theodore Barris, *Fire Canoe* (Toronto, 1976), 24-25.
4.   Stanley, 104-109.
5.   H.T. Johnston, *History of Presbyterianism in Thunder Bay and District, 1869-1980* (Thunder Bay, 1982), 4.
6.   Alexander Topp, *The Home and Foreign Record of the Canada Presbyterian Church,* Oct. 1870.
7.   James Nisbet, *The Home and Foreign Record of the Canada Presbyterian Church,* Oct. 1870
8.   *Ibid.,* 34.
9.   *Ibid.*
10. R.A. Dunning, *A Century of Presbyterianism in Saskatchewan, 1866-1966,* 13-15.
11. D. Gunn and R. Tuttle, *History of Red River: Sketch of the Life of Donald Gunn* (Ottawa, 1880).
12. *Pioneers,* 189.
13. UCA, *Presbytery Minutes, 1870-1875,* 2.

Chapter Seven: The Period of the Prebytery of Manitoba, 1870-1884

1.   *Pioneers,* 6-7.
2.   Morton, 145.
3.   *Ibid.,* 147.
4.   Moir, 90.

5. *Ibid.*, 137-138.
6. Alexander Morris, *The Treaties of Canada with the Indians, 1880* (Toronto, 1880), 106.
7. *Ibid.*

Chapter 8: The Indians, the Crown and the Church

1. Morris, 296-97.
2. *Ibid.*
3. *Ibid.*
4. Gerald Friesen, *The Canadian Prairies: A History* (Toronto, 1984), 157-158.
5. P.L. Neufeld, 'George and Mary Flett: Forming the Faith on the Frontier', *Presbyterian Record* (Jan. 1975), 15.
6. *Ibid.*
7. *Ibid.*
8. Dunning, 19.
9. *Ibid.*, 20-24.

Chapter 9: Manitoba College: Its Beginnings and Development, 1870-1884

1. *Synod of Manitoba Minutes* (Winnipeg, 1920), 22-23.
2. A.G. Bedford, *The University of Winnipeg: A History of the Founding Colleges* (Toronto, 1976), 6.
3. *Pioneers*, 96.
4. Bedford, 7-8.
5. Morton, 169-170.
6. Bedford, 22-23.
7. *Ibid.*, quoting from 'General Assembly Proceedings 1874', Appendix, 95, 7-8.
8. Hugh McKellar, *Presbyterian Pioneer Missionaries in Manitoba, Saskatchewan, Alberta, and British Columbia* (Toronto 1924), 37-38.
9. Bedford, quoting from A.B. Baird's 'History of the University of Manitoba', in *Lodge Essays*, 22-23), 12.
10. *Ibid.*, 16-17.
11. *Pioneers*, 116.
12. *Synod of Manitoba Minutes* (1922), 22-23.

Chapter 10: Finding Presbyterians: The Home Mission, 1871-1884

1. Friesen, 157-158.

SELECTED BIBLIOGRAPHY

PRIMARY SOURCES

MANUSCRIPTS
Metropolitan Toronto Library Board, Toronto.
    Lord Selkirk Papers.
Provincial Archives of Manitoba, Winnipeg.
    Alexander Ross Papers.
    Thomas Douglas Selkirk Papers.
United Church Archives, Winnipeg.
    Presbytery Minutes, 1870-75.
University of Winnipeg Archives, Winnipeg.
    John Black Letters.

SECONDARY SOURCES

Barris, Theodore. *Fire Canoe*. Toronto: McClelland and Stewart, 1977.

Bedford, A.G. *The University of Winnipeg: A History of the Founding Colleges*. Toronto: University of Toronto Press, 1976.

Bond, J.W. ed., "Minnesota and its Resources," W.L. Morton, *Introduction to Eden Colvile's Letters 1849-52*. London: Hudson Bay Record Society, 1956.

Bryce, George. *Life of Lord Selkirk*. Toronto: Musson, 1912.

———. *John Black, The Apostle of the Red River*. Toronto: William Briggs, 1898.

Butcher, W.L., et al. eds. *Prairie Spirit: Perspectives on the Heritage of the United Church of Canada in the West*. Winnipeg: University of Manitoba Press, 1985.

Canada Presbyterian Church. General Assembly Proceedings, 1874.

Dunning, R.A. *A Century of Presbyterianism in Saskatchewan*. Prince Albert, SK: St. Paul's Presbyterian Church, 1966.

Farris, A.L., Markell, H. Keith, and Smith, Neil G. *A Short History of the Presbyterian Church in Canada*. Toronto: Presbyterian Publications, 1975.

Friesen, Gerald. *The Canadian Prairies*. Toronto: University of Toronto Press, 1984.

Gunn, Donald. *History of Manitoba from the Earliest Settlement to 1835*. Ottawa: Maclean Roger, 1880.

Haig, Kenneth M. *What Mean These Stones?* Winnipeg: Kildonan Presbyterian Church, 1951.

Henderson, Anne M. *Kildonan on the Red*. Winnipeg: Winnipeg Lord Selkirk Association of Rupertsland, 1981.

Johnston, H.T. *History of Presbyterianism in Thunder Bay and District 1869-1980*. Thunder Bay, ON, 1982.

Jones, D.O. "Knox Presbyterian Church, Oakville Part II." *Presbyterian History*, XXVI (October 1982).

Martin, Chester B. *Lord Selkirk's Work in Canada*. Oxford: Clarendon Press, 1916.

McBeth, M.E. *The Old Stone Church—The History Little Britain United Church*. Winnipeg: Manitoba Historic Resources Branch, reprinted 1984.

——. *The Story of Kildonan Church 1851-1951*. Winnipeg: Manitoba Historic Resources Branch, reprinted 1984.

McKellar, Hugh. *Presbyterian Pioneer Missionaries in Manitoba, Saskatchewan, Alberta, and British Columbia*. Toronto: Murray Printing Co., 1924.

Moir, John S. "Enduring Witness," *A History of the Presbyterian Church in Canada*. Toronto: Presbyterian Church in Canada, 1974.

Morton, W.L. *Manitoba: A History*. Toronto: University of Toronto Press, 1957.

Morris, Alexander. *The Treaties of Canada with the Indians*. Toronto: Belfords Clarke and Publishers Co., 1880.

Mulligan, Helen and Ryder, Wanda. *Ghost Towns of Manitoba*. Surrey, BC: Heritage House Publishing Co., 1985.

Nisbet, J. *The Home and Foreign Record of the Canada Presbyterian Church*. (October 1870).

Neufeld, P.L. "George and Mary Flett: Forming the Faith on the Frontier." *Presbyterian Record*, Toronto (January 1975).

——. "John Tanner." *Presbyterian Record*, Toronto (September 1978).

Pioneers and Early Citizens of Manitoba: A Dictionary of Manitoba Biography from the Earliest Times to 1920. Winnipeg: Manitoba Libarary Association, 1971.

Pritchett, J.P. *The Red River Valley 1811-1849.* New Haven: Yale University Press, 1942.

Reid, W. Stanford, ed. *The Scottish Tradition in Canada.* Toronto: McClelland and Stewart in association with the Multiculturalism Program Dept. of the Secretary of State of Canada and the Publishing Centre, Supply and Services Canada, 1976.

Ross, Alexander. *The Red River Settlement.* London: Smith Elder and Co., 1856.

Stanley, G.H.G. *Louis Riel.* Toronto: Ryerson Press, 1963.

Strathclair, Rural Municipality of. *Our Story to 1970.* Strathclair, MB: 1970.

Sutherland, Alexander H. *The Selkirk Settlement in Red River.* Self-published, undated.

Thompson, Albert E. *Chief Peguis and His Descendants.* Winnipeg: Peguis Publishers, 1973.

Topp, Alexander. *The Home and Foreign Record of the Canadian Presbyterian Church* (October 1870).

Tuttle, Charles R. *From 1835 to the Admission of the Province with the Dominion.* Ottawa: Maclean Roger, 1880.

White, Patrick C., edited with an intro. *Lord Selkirk's Diary 1803-04.* Toronto: Champlain Society, 1958.

Wilson, Clifford. *Campbell of the Yukon.* Toronto: Macmillan, 1970.